Thomas Violet,
a Sly and Dangerous Fellow

Thomas Violet, a Sly and Dangerous Fellow

Silver and Spying in Civil War London

Amos Tubb

ROWMAN & LITTLEFIELD
Lanham • Boulder • New York • London

Published by Rowman & Littlefield
A wholly owned subsidiary of
The Rowman & Littlefield Publishing Group, Inc.
4501 Forbes Boulevard, Suite 200, Lanham, Maryland 20706
https://rowman.com

Unit A, Whitacre Mews, 26-34 Stannary Street, London SE11 4AB,
United Kingdom

British Library Cataloguing in Publication Information Available

Library of Congress Cataloging-in-Publication Data Available
ISBN 978-1-4422-7505-8 (hardback : alk. paper)
ISBN 978-1-4422-7506-5 (pbk. : alk. paper)
ISBN 978-1-4422-7507-2 (electronic)

∞ ™ The paper used in this publication meets the minimum requirements of American
National Standard for Information Sciences Permanence of Paper for Printed Library
Materials, ANSI/NISO Z39.48-1992.

Printed in the United States of America

Contents

Acknowledgments   vii

Maps   ix

Author's Note   xvii

Introduction   1

1   Goldsmith   9

2   Spy   23

3   Royalist   39

4   Economist   53

5   Trappaner   75

6   Republican   87

7   Anti-Semite   105

8   Roman   119

Conclusion   133

Bibliography   145

Index   151

About the Author   159

Acknowledgments

I would like to take this opportunity to thank the people who have helped me to finish this book. First of all, since this is a book primarily for college students, I would like to thank all of my students at Centre College, particularly those who were with me in London in 2014 and those who took British history with me in 2015–16, who read parts of the manuscript. The book could not have been written without Centre's study abroad program to London. It was there in 2008, as director of the program, that I first came across Violet in the British Library. Centre's interlibrary loan librarian, Carrie Frey, was an invaluable help throughout the process. My colleagues at Centre, Lee Jefferson, John Kinkade, Judith Jia, John Perry, Jim Morrison, and Bruce Johnson, have heard far more about Violet than anyone needs to. David Randall, Nicole Greenspan, Rob Hermann, Caroline Boswell, and Nat Wood have been a source of much support and many useful insights. Tom Cogswell reminded me in 2011 that I needed to keep looking for archival sources about Violet, and because of that quest I found Violet's suicide note. Thanks to Marie Petkus and Ravi Radhakrishnan for reading chapter 4. Steve Beaudoin has not only read much of the manuscript, his feedback has also dramatically improved it. Maren Anton, Sharon Tubb, Karen Tubb, and Lonnie Harp deserve special thanks for reading the entire manuscript and giving me many useful tips.

At Rowman & Littlefield, Susan McEachern has been a steady hand and a helpful guide. I would also like to thank the anonymous reviewers of the book, who took the time to give me very constructive criticism.

Eleanor, Henry, and George finally get to see Daddy's book. If the cover is scary, I'm sorry.

It almost doesn't need to be said, but the book is dedicated to Karen.

Maps

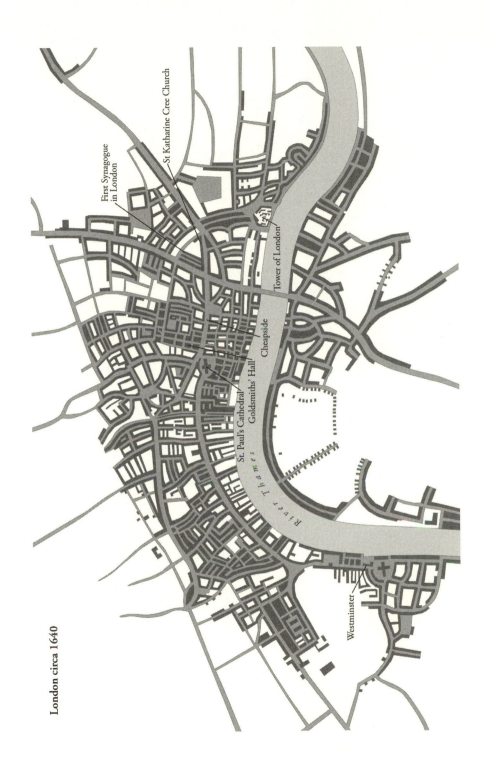

London circa 1640

First Synagogue in London

St Katharine Cree Church

Tower of London

St. Paul's Cathedral

Goldsmiths' Hall

Cheapside

River Thames

Westminster

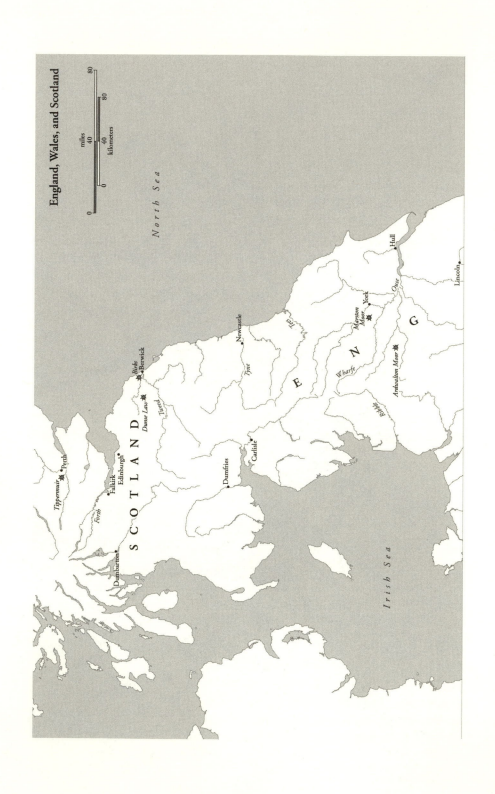

England, Wales, and Scotland

miles
0   40   80

0   40   80
kilometers

North Sea

Irish Sea

SCOTLAND

ENG

Perth
Tippermuir

Dumbarton

Falkirk
Edinburgh
Forth

Dunse Law

Berwick
Birks

Tweed

Dumfries

Carlisle

Newcastle

Tyne

Tees

Wharfe

York
Marston Moor

Ribble

Adwalton Moor

Ouse

Hull

Lincoln

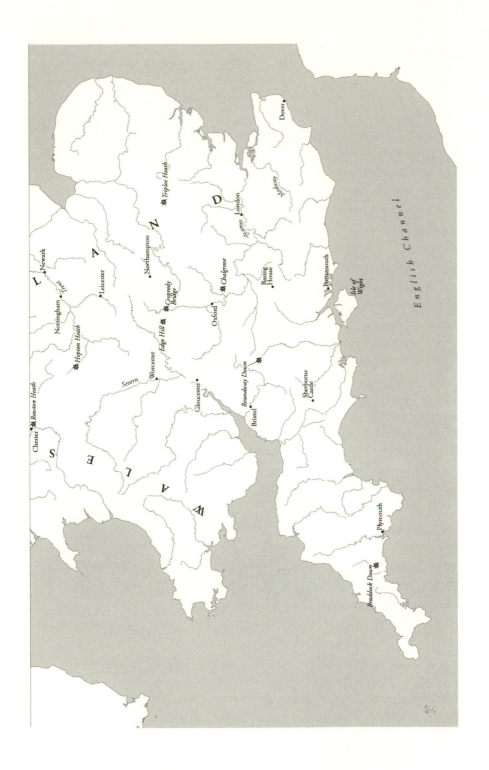

English Channel

Dover

Medway

Thames

London

Triple Heath

N

D

Portsmouth

Isle of Wight

Chalgrove

Basing House

Northampton

Cropredy Bridge

A

Newark

L

Leicester

Trent

Oxford

Nottingham

Hopton Heath

Edge Hill

Worcester

Severn

Roundway Down

Sherborne Castle

Chester

Rowton Heath

Gloucester

Bristol

S

E

L

A

W

Plymouth

Braddock Down

England and Wales
at the Outbreak of
the Civil War

Districts and places held by the King
Districts and places held by Parliament

North Sea

Irish Sea

Northumberland

Newcastle

Cumberland   Durham

Westmorland

York   York

Leeds

Lancaster   Hull

Anglesey   Flint   Lincoln   Lincoln
Carnarvon   Denbigh   Chester   Chester   Derby
                                                    Nottingham   Newark
Merioneth   Nottingham
                              Stafford   *Trent*
Montgomery   Salop   Leicester   Norfolk   Norwich
                                 Leicester   Rutland
Cardigan   Radnor   Warwick   Northampton   Huntingdon
                  Hereford   Worcester   Northampton   Suffolk
Carmarthen Brecknock   Worcester   Bedford
                            Severn   Cambridge
Pembroke   Buckingham   Hertford
          Glamorgan   Monmouth   Gloucester   Oxford Oxford   Essex
                            Gloucester   Middlesex *Thames*
                      Bristol   Berks   London
                                                       Surrey   Kent
                              Wilts   Basing House   Dover
          Somerset   Hants
                   Sherborne   Portsmouth   Sussex
                   Castle
          Devon   Dorset   *Isle of
                                                    Wight*
Cornwall   Plymouth

English Channel

miles
0   50   100
0   50   100
kilometers

England and Wales
after the
Campaigns of 1644

Districts and places held by the King
Districts and places held by Parliament

North Sea

Northumberland

Newcastle

Cumberland

Durham

Westmorland

E
N
G

York York

Leeds

Hull

Irish Sea

Lancaster

Anglesey Flint

Carnarvon Denbigh

Chester
Chester

Derby

L
I

Lincoln Lincoln

Merioneth

Stafford

Nottingham Newark

Nottingham

Trent

Montgomery

Salop

Leicester

Leicester

Rutland

Norfolk Norwich

W
A
L
E
S

Radnor

Cardigan

Worcester

Warwick

Northampton

Northampton

Huntingdon

Cambridge

Suffolk

Hereford

Worcester

Pembroke

Carmarthen

Brecknock

Bedford

N
D

Glamorgan

Monmouth

Gloucester

Oxford

Buckingham

Hertford

Essex

Gloucester

Oxford

Middlesex

Thames

London

Berks

Basing House

Surrey

Kent

Bristol

Wilts

Dover

Somerset

Hants

Sussex

Sherborne
Castle

Portsmouth

Devon

Dorset

*Isle of
Wight*

Cornwall

Plymouth

English Channel

miles
0   50   100

0   50   100
kilometers

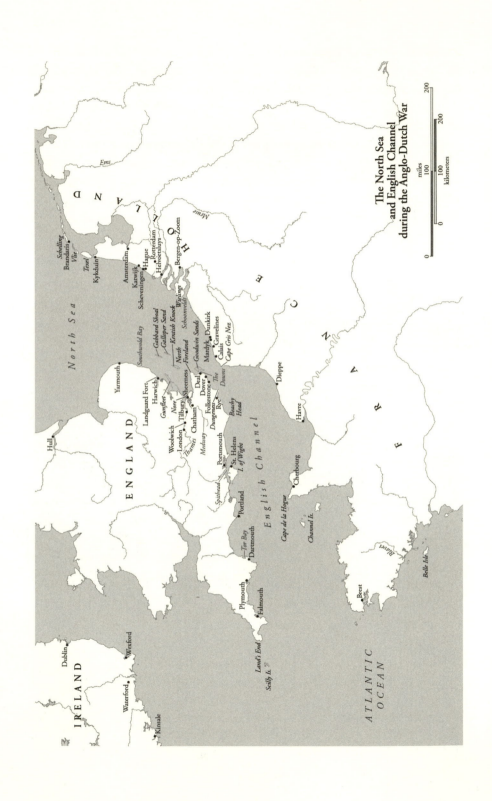

The North Sea
and English Channel
during the Anglo-Dutch War

miles
0   100   200
0   100   200
kilometers

IRELAND

Dublin
Wexford
Waterford
Kinsale

ENGLAND

Hull
Yarmouth
Southwold Bay
Landguard Fort
Harwich
Gunfleet
Nore
Woolwich
London
Tilbury
Chatham
Thames
Medway
Sheerness
Deal
Dover
Folkestone
Dungeness
Rye
The Downs
Portsmouth
St. Helens
I. of Wight
Spithead
Portland
Tor Bay
Dartmouth
Plymouth
Falmouth
Land's End
Scilly Is.

North Sea

Schelling
Brandaris
Vlie
Texel
Kykduin
Amsterdam
Karwijk
Scheveningen
Hague
Rotterdam
Helvoetsluys
Bergen-op-Zoom
Ems

HOLLAND

Meuse

Gabbard Shoal
Galliper Sand
Kentish Knock
North Foreland
Goodwin Sands
Mardyk
Dunkirk
Gravelines
Calais
Cape Gris Nez
Wieling
Schoonveldt

English Channel

Beachy Head
Dieppe
Havre
Cherbourg
Cape de la Hague
Channel Is.

FRANCE

Brest
Blavet
Belle Isle

ATLANTIC
OCEAN

Author's Note

In early modern England, the New Year began on March 25. I have taken the New Year to be January 1. I have also modernized most seventeenth-century spelling and punctuation.

Introduction

It was over. Thomas Violet could do nothing more to save himself. So far in debt that bankruptcy seemed inevitable, Violet decided to opt out. In his London home, at one o'clock in the afternoon on April 20, 1662, he chose to end his life. With just a few minutes to live, Violet continued a nearly thirty-year habit of writing down and justifying his actions. He took up his pen and wrote, "I have poisoned myself good Lord." Almost immediately he felt the fatal toxin working in his body and knew that "now the pangs of death are on me." With his hand trembling, and with only moments of life left, he begged "Christ Jesus forgiveness." Realizing that what he was doing was against all of his society's Christian beliefs, Violet pleaded to Jesus to "pray for me" and asked him to "intercede for me" to "wipe away all my sins"—especially "this great crying sin." His last act on earth was to scrawl his signature "Tho. Violet" and with that, he died. He was fifty-two.[1]

Committing suicide was just the final sin in a long list of unchristian acts accumulated over Violet's lifetime. This dying man called to Jesus in a desperate attempt for companionship but he remained utterly and completely alone, devoid of friendship. As in life, in death he chose isolation, and this decision bore its natural fruits. Violet had no mourners at his funeral—the people who cared that he had died were only creditors, enemies, and disgruntled family members. Violet earned this animosity because throughout his life he mistreated people. Although he did not abuse people physically, he spent his life ruining others by legally stealing their money. In fact, earning money at others' expense was the sole pursuit of his life.

1

Two centuries before Charles Dickens invented Ebenezer Scrooge, Violet embodied the archetype for such a character. For just like Scrooge, Violet cared more about money than his fellow man. His actions were ruthless and, more often than not, caused others grief. Over the course of his life, Violet was a banker, a smuggler, a counterfeiter, a government informant, a spy, a traitor (twice over), and an anti-Semite. All his actions demeaned, impoverished, or disgraced either an individual or a group of people.

This soulless creature had apparently almost no redeeming characteristics. He appeared to care about only two people in his entire life: his mother, Sara Violet, and Timothy Eman, the man who trained him as a teenager to be a goldsmith (an early version of the modern banker). Even then, when his mother was dying, he complained that he had to visit her and not tend to his business deals. Meanwhile, he betrayed Eman, who raised him for nine years, and ruined the man. It is little wonder that an acquaintance said, "Thomas Violet: [has] a name too sweet for so foul a carcass."[2]

Yet strangely, because he spent his life defrauding people during some of the most important events in English history, his life is worth studying. In the 1630s, King Charles I ruled England without Parliament. To do so, he needed to raise income without resorting to Parliamentary taxation. Charles relied on men like Violet, an active goldsmith from 1631–62, to find this money. Violet used his specialized knowledge of how Englishmen made, spent, and recycled coinage to prove that a wide range of people were breaking the king's currency laws and therefore could be fined. The enormous payments he netted helped fund King Charles I's regime. Then, in 1640, when Charles was forced to call a Parliament, he quarreled with it, and eventually relations between the king and Parliament grew so strained it led to the outbreak of the English Civil War in 1642. Violet decided to side with the king because he believed it would help him financially. While working as a spy for the king, though, he was captured by Parliament's forces and imprisoned for the duration of the war. After being freed, Violet switched sides and supported Parliament. In the 1650s, Violet helped Parliament stabilize England's economy and pay for its war machine. He then involved himself in an elaborate scheme to defraud and expel the Jews living in England. Finally, when Parliament's government collapsed in 1660 and King Charles II returned from exile in the Restoration, Violet declared his loyalty to the new government and attempted to use Charles II to help him destroy the Jews in England. In the end, his schemes came to naught because he angered so many people with manipulative and self-serving plots. Unable to generate any income, and with his line of credit exhausted, he killed himself to avoid bankruptcy.

This book will use each of Violet's adventurous episodes to explore and examine different aspects of seventeenth-century English society. As students of history, we are intrigued by Violet's deeds on their own merits, but they also provide entrée into several of the many contentious historiographical debates about seventeenth-century England. It should not surprise us that scholars argue so fiercely about England's history during those years because they midwifed many of the political, religious, economic, and social issues that birthed modern Britain. Since he meddled in so many different schemes, Violet can tell us about all of these themes.

The political divisions in England during Violet's lifetime were so extreme that they led to the English Civil War, which was arguably the worst war in English history—even bloodier than World War I. Its cost in lives, treasure, and property was almost unbearable. Despite years of research, scholars are divided about the people's motivations for fighting a war that almost destroyed the country. Some historians argue that the English had political and religious ideological motives for starting the war. Others say that economic tensions between emerging social classes helped create the conditions for warfare. Another group asserts that individual bonds of loyalty shaped who fought for the Royalists or Parliamentarians during the struggle. Violet shows a whole different aspect of allegiance—Violet fought for whoever would reward him more richly, be it a Royalist or Parliamentarian. Notions of political and religious beliefs had nothing to do with his decisions, and Violet, an immigrant son of a Dutch man and an Italian woman, certainly was not supporting the king for personal allegiance, nor would he support Parliamentarians for political liberty.[3]

Scholars have discussed and argued about the role of social networking in achieving financial and social success in early modern London. A lifetime denizen of the city, Violet shows us how someone who clearly held most other humans in contempt, someone who regularly violated social norms, could not only survive, but thrive in the city. Further, during the Civil War period (1640–60) the English experienced dramatic changes in print culture. For most of the 1640s, there was no effective censorship, which allowed men and women to write and publish broadsides, pamphlets, newsbooks (weekly newspapers), and books on a whole host of controversial topics. This has led to numerous scholarly debates about the nature of print in the Civil War era—how it was consumed; how it was produced; and what impact it had on the causes, course, and outcome of the wars.[4] While Violet shied away from political and religious debates, he wrote pamphlets and petitions from the 1630s through the 1660s, and his published works show how the new print culture of the mid-seventeenth century provided occasions for the son of a Dutch musician to command the attention of King Charles I, Oliver Cromwell, and King Charles II.

Violet also helps us understand the many facets of emerging English nationalism. Scholars have made convincing arguments that the English had crafted a sense of national identity by the seventeenth century (which was rather unusual in Europe at the time). What they disagree on is what made up English nationalism. Virtually all historians acknowledge that seventeenth-century Englishmen believed that to be English meant being Protestant and hating the Spanish, but historians disagree about what other definitions of Englishness mattered. For instance, it is not clear how widespread the ideas were that the rule of law, having political rights that were defended by Parliament, and the often-used, but ill-defined, term "liberty" constituted Englishness. Further, while virtually all seventeenth-century English people (and scholars) would agree that anti-Catholicism helped keep the political nation together, English attitudes toward foreigners were complex. Clearly, some people hated all foreigners, including their fellow inhabitants of the British archipelago. On the other hand, many foreigners lived happily in England for decades. Violet, in his case, attempted to exploit English prejudices against non-Protestants by trying to drive the Jews living in England out of the country in an effort to bolster his own finances. By promoting religious bigotry for his own financial reward, Violet unveils the strength of these anti-foreigner, anti-Semitic undertones developing in English nationalism during the period.[5]

Meanwhile, his suicide helps explains attitudes toward self-murder in early modern England. When Violet killed himself, suicide was not only a sin against God in Christian England, but also illegal. Yet Violet lived during a time when attitudes about suicide were rapidly changing in practice. Violet wrote in his suicide note that he was making "a Roman resolution" to take his own life. Violet, who never indicated he had any classical education, alluded to the ancient Roman practice of suicide. The pagan Romans saw suicide as a virtuous act, not a sin against God and the state. Violet copied this language because he wanted to cloak his suicide as an act of embracing popular Renaissance philosophers and their support of classical Roman thinkers. Yet his final words belie his Roman resolution: when Thomas Violet came to his end, he feared his soul would be punished for his Roman, Renaissance act. [6]

Studying Violet's life also sheds light on the field of economics. Our understanding of seventeenth-century economic policy and theory has been shaped almost entirely by Adam Smith. When the founder of modern economic thought published *The Wealth of Nations* in 1776, he introduced a new word to his readers to describe seventeenth- and eighteenth-century economies: mercantilism. Smith argued that seventeenth-century economists invented the "Mercantile System" in the 1620s. According to Smith, these writers thought that the wealth of a nation was tied to how much money—or, literally, gold and silver—was in the country. Consequently, these theorists advocated economic policies of protectionism in order to ensure that their country had a positive balance of payments. This system of protected trade was the straw man that Smith attacked in his great work. [7]

For nearly two centuries, historians took Smith at his word that this was in fact the economic system seventeenth-century thinkers advocated. In recent decades, though, scholars have argued that Smith misrepresented the economists of the seventeenth century, as well as their intellectual diversity. There was an entire school of thinkers in the seventeenth century who asserted that the problem with their economy, as they saw it, was that individual companies received government-sponsored monopolies on the trade to a specific region of the world. Instead of this system, they argued that merchants from the entire country should be free to trade with whatever part of the world they wished. Further, there were some, like Thomas Violet, who made the case that there should be free trade and open ports, where the English would allow foreign nationals the right to trade in English ports without paying exorbitant customs fees. [8]

Yet while historians have revised our understanding of the economic theories of the seventeenth century, they have by and large ignored Violet. This book will explain why. Violet's contemporaries did not trust him—and with good reason. Violet had spent his entire adult life using his specialized expertise and understanding of how the financial service industry of his time operated to enrich himself at others' expense. Violet is a three-and-a-half-century-old example of a greedy financier with a track record of using his skills to rig any economic exchange for his own benefit. Therefore, when he argued for free trade, people assumed he did not want government regulation of his activities so he could rob them without any cost to himself. No prudent Englishman would follow the ideas of "a sly and dangerous fellow" in the economic arena. Consequently, one reason he was ignored, and why his ideas did not define his generation, was that their proponent was a villain.[9]

Finally, Violet enables us to grapple with the growing phenomenon of individualism in early modern Europe. Historians have argued that during the Italian Renaissance and Protestant Reformation, Europeans began to create a new sense of self. Instead of communal values, in which the larger society or family mattered more than the individual, early modern Europeans began to imagine a world in which individuals, and their rights and achievements, were worth celebrating. Often, scholars denote the idea of the development of the sense of self and individualism as the beginning of the modern era, when humans could strive to create art, develop new scientific ideas, and eventually lay the foundations of political liberty in the Enlightenment. While this insight is no doubt correct, Violet reveals the opposite impact of the growing sense of individualism. It allows people to be completely selfish and ignore the effect their actions have on others. Instead of inspiring the rest of humanity, individualism gave Violet carte blanche to defraud it.[10]

Violet thus helps us understand many different aspects of England's history during the country's most difficult trial. While *A Sly and Dangerous Fellow* is Violet's biography, and each of its chapters describes a particular time in his life, it will use his life as a vehicle to help better understand the society Violet lived in. By doing so, perhaps you will be able to see how individuals can both shape and be shaped by the times in which they live.

NOTES

1. National Archives, Records of the Prerogative Court of Canterbury (PROB) 20/2650, 5th sheet. Seventeenth-century spellings have been modernized for clarity.

2. Anon., *The Great Trappanner of England Discovered* (London, 1660), 1.

3. See Michael Braddick, *God's Fury, England's Fire: A New History of the English Civil Wars* (London: Allen Lane, 2008), 224–36, for an overview of choosing sides.

4. Ann Hughes, *Gangraena and the Struggle for the English Revolution* (Oxford: Oxford University Press, 2004); Joad Raymond, *The Invention of the Newspaper: English Newsbooks 1641–1649* (Oxford: Oxford University Press, 1996); Jason McElligott, *Royalism, Print and Censorship in Revolutionary England* (Woodbridge, UK: Boydell Press, 2007); Jason Peacey, *Politicians and Pamphleteers: Propaganda During the English Civil Wars and Interregnum* (Aldershot, UK: Ashgate, 2004); Jason Peacey, *Print and Public Politics in the English Revolution* (Cambridge: Cambridge University Press, 2013).

5. For a positive view of English nationalism in the sixteenth and seventeenth centuries, see George Yerby, *The English Revolution and the Roots of Environmental Change* (New York: Routledge, 2016). For a more negative view, see Mark Stoyle, *Soldiers & Strangers: An Ethnic History of the English Civil War* (New Haven, CT: Yale University Press, 2005). See

David Katz, *The Jews in the History of England 1485–1850* (Oxford: Oxford University Press, 1994) for an engaging, single-volume introduction to Jewish history during the period.

6. See Michael MacDonald and Terence R. Murphy, *Sleepless Souls: Suicide in Early Modern England* (Oxford: Oxford University Press, 1990) for an outstanding introduction to this topic.

7. Adam Smith, *The Wealth of Nations* (1776, repr., New York: Bantam Dell, 2003).

8. See Carl Wennerlind, "Money: Hartlibian Political Economy and the New Culture of Credit," in *Mercantilism Reimagined: Political Economy in Early Modern Britain and Its Empire*, eds. Philip J. Stern and Carl Wennerlind (Oxford: Oxford University Press, 2014), 74–77, for an excellent summary of these issues. See also Smith, *The Wealth of Nations*.

9. Thomas Violet, *An Appeal to Caesar* (London, 1662), 54.

10. A good place to start with this literature is Christopher Lasch, *The Culture of Narcissism* (New York: W. W. Norton, 1978); David Sabean, *Power in the Blood* (Cambridge: Cambridge University Press, 1988); and Peter Stearns and Carol Stearns, eds., *Emotion and Social Change: Toward a New Psychohistory* (New York: Holmes & Meier, 1988).

Chapter One

Goldsmith

Throughout his adult life, Thomas Violet strove for one thing above all others—money. Yet for Violet, a business deal was almost never a situation where both parties benefited. It was instead an opportunity for him to fool, trap, swindle, fine, or humiliate the man he was trading with. While Violet's unsavory goals, character, and methods cannot be blamed entirely on his early environment, it is likely that his childhood experiences helped shape his desires and his notion of the appropriate way to treat people. Two important facts dominated Thomas Violet's childhood—his parents' relative poverty and the fact that both were immigrants. His father, Peter Vyolett, was born in Antwerp in what was then the Spanish Netherlands. A musician, Peter had to travel in order to earn his living, bringing him in contact with people throughout Europe. One of these connections introduced Peter to his future wife, an Italian woman named Sara Dyamont. Peter and Sara Vyolett had at least four children: Peter, John, Thomas, and a girl whose name they never recorded. Sometime around Thomas Violet's birth (probably in 1609), Peter and Sara decided that life would be better in London and moved their family from Antwerp to the English metropolis. It is not clear if Thomas was born before or after they moved; he may have even arrived when the family was crossing the English Channel. Wherever he was born, Thomas Violet was baptized in London on December 5, 1609.

As the child of a Dutch musician and an Italian woman so dark skinned that acquaintances wondered if she was African, Violet would have always been an outsider, even in relatively cosmopolitan London. While seventeenth-century Britons had not yet developed the racist attitudes of the eight-

9

eenth century, they certainly noticed differences in skin color. Violet's childhood was likely marked by taunts about his foreign parents and particularly
his "Moorish" mother. If being insulted about his parentage was not enough
to make him feel like an outsider, London's busy streets would have provided constant reminders of his poverty. Unlike in modern cities where rich
and poor live in different areas, in seventeenth-century London, the wealthy,
the middle sort, and the poor lived cheek by jowl. Within a few yards of his
modest dwelling he saw wealthy merchants who resided in grand homes, had
dozens of servants, and lived a far better life than his musician father could
ever hope to achieve. Violet's family lived in an eastern section of the city in
a parish called St. Katharine Creechurch. Young Thomas spent his youth
going to church on Leadenhall Street, just down the road from where many
of the wealthiest businessmen in London lived. These merchants' craft had
generated almost unimaginable levels of wealth. They represented everything Thomas wanted: instead of being poor and foreign, they were rich,
powerful, and English. They were called goldsmiths.[1]

Goldsmiths earned their wealth and influence by participating in three
critical activities that shaped England's economy. First, they worked with
gold and silver as craftsmen. By transforming gold and silver bullion into
beautiful jewelry or servingware (called plate), they increased the value of
the metals. During the Middle Ages, goldsmiths realized that they could use
the gold that they stored in their shops as collateral for loans. They quickly
moved into the businesses of pawnbroking, moneylending, and, finally,
banking. They added to these lucrative activities in the thirteenth century
when their public corporation, the Goldsmiths' Company, became an integral
participant in the creation of money. Before the invention of paper money,
gold and silver coins comprised all English currency. Goldsmiths minted the
coins for the government at the Royal Mint in the Tower of London, the
medieval fortress at the edge of the city. The Goldsmiths' Company was
responsible for quality control and preventing counterfeiting. Ironically,
since they were the only ones who knew how to make money, they were also
the most likely counterfeiters. By the early seventeenth century, goldsmiths
both policed and stole the government's currency. Because of these developments, the Goldsmiths' Company oversaw a very lucrative trade, but one
dominated by men of dubious morality.[2]

It is little wonder that a poor boy with ambition only for money, and who
lived down the street from the goldsmiths, would see them as his ticket to
prosperity. Thomas Violet never reveals when he decided he wanted to be a

goldsmith, but he was very young when he started on the path. He became an apprentice to goldsmith Timothy Eman on January 18, 1622, when Violet was about thirteen. He moved to Lombard Street to live with his master. Becoming an apprentice for an incredibly successful goldsmith would not have been easy, and Violet is not forthcoming about how he, or more likely his parents, managed to get him this coveted position. It may be that Eman felt sorry for the little Dutch/Italian boy. Eman, although a wealthy goldsmith, had been born in the English countryside and may have seen himself in the young immigrant. He treated Violet kindly and Violet always spoke of him with affection. Eman of course was not only generous to Violet personally; he also set him on the path to riches. For by becoming Eman's apprentice, Violet earned the right to live with his master for most of a decade, learn the trade, develop business contacts, and then start his life as a journeyman and eventually a master goldsmith. By moving a short way down Lombard Street, Violet had taken a large step up in the world and, almost immediately, he could see what goldsmiths did: handle vast sums of money and then skim as much off the top as they could without anyone's noticing.[3]

It was an exciting time for the young man, and it is possible that during this period Thomas Vyolett started spelling his name like an Englishman— either Thomas Violett or Thomas Violet. Britons at the time were lax about spelling, even of their own names, and Violet was simply following convention by spelling his own with one "t" or two. In either case, by Anglicizing his name, he announced to the world that he was no longer a Dutch immigrant, but an Englishman. Further, he was an Englishman embarking on a career that could lead him to uncounted riches. It was a new world and he needed to acknowledge that with a new name.[4]

As soon as he started working for Timothy Eman, Violet was introduced to the magic of goldsmithing: making money from money. There were several ways goldsmiths did this—for instance, lending money at high interest— but that tended to be rather unpopular. A more subtle way to make money from money was to use their specialized knowledge of coins to create bullion out of gold and silver coins without destroying the coins. Goldsmiths understood that each gold and silver coin was supposed to weigh a certain amount. However, because of mistakes in the production process, a sizable percentage of coins actually weighed more than they should have. Goldsmiths learned that by shaving off the edges of these coins they could literally make money from money. For instance, if a goldsmith shaved even one pound off of

£1,000 of gold coins, he still had the £1,000 of gold coins, but he would also now have an additional pile of gold bullion worth about £40.[5]

Goldsmiths had been doing this for hundreds of years by the time Violet became an apprentice. Violet learned the skill from his master, a leading member of a group of ten important goldsmiths in London who, from 1621 to 1631, generated a profit of at least £85,000 by tampering with coins.[6] To put Eman's scam in perspective, the English government's total debt in 1635 was only £1,000,000.[7] Eman's methods were straightforward. He used his position as a goldsmith to act as a banker for merchants' money. Eman then had his apprentices, including Violet, measure and organize the coins he had received as deposits by weight. He found the "heaviest shillings and six-pences, and afterwards sold them by the ounce." Eman earned "three pound in the hundred pound" on the scam. In short, he took coins that were supposed to weigh 100 pounds and resold them (in different guises) as if they weighed 103 pounds. By the end of the 1620s Eman and his partners were so good at this that they "culled," as they called it, £500,000 worth of coins a year. They then melted the shavings of these coins down into gold ingots and sold them for a value of £20,000. Eman's own cut from this was somewhat smaller. Between 1621 and 1626 he melted down £5,000 a year and from 1626 to 1631, he melted £15,000 a year, earning £1,000 a year in profit.[8]

Eman's partners included a goldsmith named Henry Flutter, who regularly brought in extra gold and silver for Eman's servants to melt down. While there were many others involved in Eman's scheme, Violet became closest to Flutter. The two often spoke about other ways they could make money, and in 1631, when Violet finished his apprenticeship, they became partners. Violet and Flutter had both seen the handsome profits Eman made by melting down heavy coins, but Eman's trade was well covered by London's goldsmiths. Violet and Flutter consequently agreed on a different strategy for making money from money. They decided to trade English coins for foreign coins and earn money on the exchange rate. The problem with this plan was that the English government frowned on goldsmiths exporting precious metals. Due to economic difficulties in the 1620s (which will be explained more fully in chapter 4) the English government decided that any activity that exported gold and silver was deemed dangerous and bad because it believed the amount of gold and silver a nation possessed determined its wealth. Demonstrating its concern with losing money overseas, the English government passed a law in 1627 that decreed transporting money out of the kingdom a crime.[9]

Goldsmiths, on the other hand, knew that sometimes shipping money out of the country could make money. If fact, the goldsmiths who participated in international currency exchanges earned some of the largest profits in their profession. However, in order to do this, they needed a large supply of gold or silver coins as well as specialized knowledge of exchange rates. Flutter provided the gold, £1,000, and Violet the skills.[10] Befitting an ambitious, young financial operative, Violet had built contacts with French merchants in Dover, Calais, and even in Paris. When working for Eman, Violet observed that English goldsmiths came to Calais (or to French merchants in Dover) about once a month. There, they or their agents bought and sold coins from all over Europe. By recognizing which coins were worth more than others, merchants could earn substantial profits. Violet recognized that each individual who bought and sold coins had to guess (or know) the alleged value of each of the coins involved. He also had to have an idea of the actual metals used and the weight of each coin he was buying. With scores of little city-states, as well as nation-states, minting coins in Europe, a man needed almost overwhelming amounts of intelligence to earn money in currency trades.[11] Violet knew that it was better to avoid exotic trades in currency and focus on a single type of currency one could know very well. For Violet, that currency was the French coin called the *cardecu*.[12]

Violet liked the cardecu because it often was produced with more silver in it than the coin itself was actually worth. Further, in the early 1630s the cardecu was widely circulated "amongst the Bankers" in Calais, Paris, and other cities of northwest France. Violet realized that these men suffered from a surplus of silver and would trade their plentiful silver coins for gold. He took Flutter's gold to France, where he exchanged it for French silver. He made "twenty in the hundred" in his transactions, an incredible profit.[13] They were so successful that Flutter became the largest importer of silver in England—between 1632 and 1636 he imported £301,131 of silver. Both young goldsmiths had learned their trade well and were on their way to incredible riches.[14]

In many ways, these early years were the best of Violet's professional life. He used the skills and connections he developed working under Eman to become a successful goldsmith who operated a highly lucrative international business. He was a charming and witty conversationalist who was usually able to steer a business encounter to his own benefit because he could manipulate others into thinking he cared for them. Yet ultimately he could never hide his disregard for people and his preference for money over human relationships. In the early 1630s, the combination of his technical abilities at working precious metals along with his ability to read and manipulate people encouraged Violet to reveal his arrogant and disdainful attitude toward his peers. He began to mock his fellow goldsmiths, even neglecting his responsibilities as a member of the Goldsmiths' Company. Violet's actions irritated the members of the company. While making money was something they could support, attacking each other was not something they would ever condone.

The goldsmiths tried very hard to make their company a fraternity where the members enjoyed each other's fellowship and took care of one another. The Goldsmiths' Company's members often ate meals at their meetings to facilitate camaraderie and fellowship, focusing more on food and drink than actual business. Indeed, even when they were dealing with the king's pressing matters, they would stop to praise their cook's artichoke dishes. They usually managed to get the work done for their guild by asking for volunteers to stand for election, and they raised all the money for their new Goldsmiths' Hall by subscription. Yet Violet did not participate in this fellowship. In 1631, the Goldsmiths' Company "accused [him] of disrespectful words against the Warden [leader]." Then, in early 1634, when he skipped one of the company's important dinners, he was called to account and forced to pay a fine.[15]

Instead of learning to hide his contempt for others and cooperate with his peers and neighbors, these humiliations taught Violet that he did not want to be under anyone's oversight and he decided to control any future business partnership. While he continued working with Flutter, Violet began to diversify his own business relationships, reaching out to a new group: the gold and silver wire drawers of London.

Gold and silver wire drawers turned precious metal into thread to cater to the fashion for wealthy Englishmen to have gold and silver thread sewn into the fabric of their clothes. In order to make such fine material, gold and silver wire drawers needed a host of specialized equipment: hammers, anvils, pincers, tongs, rollers, files, and draw plates. It was a difficult and specific skill that resided with a small band of artisans. In Violet's time there were only thirty in London. These men piqued Violet's interest because of the quantity of gold and silver involved in the production of gold and silver thread. Theirs was also a heavily regulated industry because the production process led to wasted gold and silver. Since the government believed that destroying precious metals impoverished the country, it oversaw the drawers' work closely.

Consequently, gold and silver wire drawers had to prove that they were only processing gold and silver for their own purposes and not destroying it for illegitimate gain. Yet Violet saw that he could help the wire drawers make more money from their gold and silver by trading it on the international market than they could earn by turning it into thread. Finding a common cause, it appears these were the people Violet contacted after he insulted the city's leading goldsmiths in 1631.[16]

Violet's connections with the gold and silver wire drawers expanded in the years from 1632 to 1634. Violet probably started buying gold from the gold and silver wire drawers with French cardecus. While it is not exactly clear from the records what deal Violet offered the wire drawers, he could afford to pay a premium for English gold because he could sell it in France for a 20 percent profit. If this was the nature of their business relationship, Violet continued to make money from the French while the gold and silver wire drawers profited by selling their gold to Violet rather than turning it into gold wire.[17]

This scenario, if true, explains the events that occurred between March and April 1634 that changed Violet's career. Because the gold and silver wire drawers were buying gold and selling the gold at a profit to Violet, they started to act more like bankers and investors than simple craftsmen. The goldsmiths viewed this development with alarm because they were already the bankers of early modern England. Moving quickly to respond to this major financial threat, on March 8, 1634, a group of goldsmiths reported Violet's activities to the Council of State, which was the organization that ran the day-to-day affairs of the kingdom for the monarch. The goldsmiths wanted the Council of State to stop the gold and silver wire drawers from pushing into their business.[18] The allegation had two immediate ramifications. First, it ended an effort by the gold and silver wire drawers to gain their own charter from the king and form their own company—like the Goldsmiths' Company. Second, Thomas Violet was arrested and brought before the Star Chamber.

The Star Chamber was a special tribunal long used by English monarchs. Under King Henry VIII in the sixteenth century, it became one of the most important courts in the English judicial system.[19] In effect it was the monarch's private court where the judges and jury were all the same men—members of the king's Privy Council (which was a group of the king's private councilors).[20] The Star Chamber gave the monarch a court where he could easily control the outcome of a trial. When Violet was brought into the

Star Chamber, sitting at the council table in the middle of the room was the terrifying personage of the Secretary of State, Sir John Coke. Coke, one of the key ministers in the government, held the power of life or death over Thomas Violet. Yet despite Coke's authority, Violet felt free to defy Coke because he doubted the government had any evidence it could use against him. The only way Coke's agents could have acquired proof of his illegal acts would have been for one of Violet's colleagues to have turned him in. Since everyone involved with exporting gold and silver out of the country broke the law, almost all of Violet's business partners were criminals. He could not imagine that anyone would betray him by admitting their own guilt.[21]

Violet boldly stood up to the Secretary of State and stared him down in a setting where the English monarch's power reigned supreme. Coke, though, did not become Secretary of State by putting himself in losing situations. He sent Violet away to stew in a cell for a month. In April 1634 Coke called Violet back and told him that he wanted a confession. Violet again refused. Coke then laid out the case against Violet. He told Violet that he knew where he bought gold in London and to whom he sold it in France. Violet could not believe that the king's agents could possess such exact intelligence about his affairs. Then he realized that to know these details the government agents had to have read his business letters. The only people who could have provided them were his business partners. They had clearly sold him out to save their own skins. Yet at this point only two men had betrayed Violet. All of the rest of the men he worked with had not, as yet, provided the state with any evidence.[22]

Coke then told Violet he had one last chance to confess and come clean. Coke informed Violet he would give him fifteen minutes to tell him everything or Violet could face unimaginable horrors. Since torture was an option in prisoner interrogations in seventeenth-century England, Violet trembled. He knew he had been betrayed and that the only way to avoid unbearable punishment was to confess. Violet admitted to everything. He explained how he had illegally transported gold out of the country and who helped him do it. He told Coke how he met and worked with Henry Flutter. Finally, Violet even went so far as to explain the scam his former master Timothy Eman had run while Violet was an apprentice for him. This was very hard for Violet to do, because Eman had been very close to him and had helped him enter the goldsmith profession. Yet when faced with the prospect of suffering for other people or saving himself, Violet chose himself. Pleased with his testimony, the secretary released him and granted a full pardon after he paid a £2,000 fine.[23]

Violet had time to consider the implications of his actions. While he had insulted and ignored the Goldsmiths' Company since he became his own man, being a goldsmith was the most important part of his life. It was how he identified himself—Thomas Violet, goldsmith. Yet he had betrayed all of his business associates and even his own former master, a man who had housed him for nine years. Violet just could not imagine facing any of these men, particularly Eman. Violet saw Eman, Flutter, and the other men he betrayed nearly every day because they almost all lived on Lombard Street. Violet realized that everyone he saw would hate him, humiliate him, and maybe worst of all, no longer do business with him. He decided he could not face that prospect. He needed a way out. The twenty-five-year-old decided there was only one option: he took a "resolution to die." Into his broth, Violet poured "a dram of mercury and swallowed it." He fell immediately ill.[24]

When Violet's mother, Sara, checked on her distraught son, she saw his discolored spoon and, realizing why he was sick, rushed out to call a doctor. Together, they nursed Violet back to health. It took him twenty weeks to recuperate, enduring terrible pain the entire time. During Violet's convalescence he wondered why God allowed him to survive. He decided that the Lord had spared him because he had done the right thing in confessing and selling out all his business associates. Violet realized by this time, the end of 1634, that he might make a career of informing on his fellow goldsmiths. While he regretted betraying Eman, Violet consoled himself with the hope that by partnering with the government he could make himself one of, if not the wealthiest, goldsmiths in London.[25] He could face being a social pariah as long as he could continue making money.

At the same time, the leaders of the government began to see a way that they could use Violet for their own purposes. Throughout Violet's recovery, Secretary Coke and King Charles I (r. 1625–49) discussed the problems of the king's goldsmiths. Charles realized that his goldsmiths were defrauding him and resolved to eliminate this affront to the crown. The king's solution would be an unworkable disaster. As chapter 3 of this book will reveal, Charles was terrible at formulating political policies. He was also a dreadful politician. Charles did not possess the social skills necessary to engender loyalty, but he demanded complete obedience from his subjects. This led him to make rash, one-sided decisions that irritated his people. Further, Charles relied on grasping men like Violet to do his bidding, further damaging his own credibility. All of his faults were displayed in his plan for dealing with his goldsmiths.

Thanks to Violet's testimony, it was undeniably clear to Charles that almost all of the members of the company were corrupt and systematically defrauding his government and, by extension, his subjects.[26] The goldsmiths had long been a problem, but different English monarchs had successfully exerted control over them in the past. An accomplished politician like Elizabeth I (r. 1558–1603) simply bribed and charmed them into doing what she wanted.[27] A different type of leader, like Henry VIII (r. 1509–47), allowed them their peccadillos but then extorted money from them whenever he felt like it.[28] Charles, though, was neither as smooth as Elizabeth nor as intimidating as Henry. His own weak personality made his solution to the problem of rampant corruption among the goldsmiths all the more unenforceable.

In November 1634, he demanded that the goldsmiths all move their shops to two streets: Cheapside and Lombard. On the one hand, this made sense. Most goldsmiths lived there already and Charles believed that if they all resided there he could better supervise them. He felt that the goldsmiths living in other parts of the city were doing all sorts of illegal activities, not the least of which was "passing away of stolen plate."[29]

There were several problems with his solution. First of all, there were already people using the shops where he wanted the goldsmiths to move. For instance, there were "at least 24 houses and shops that are not inhabited by goldsmiths" on those streets.[30] Existing residents included stationers, a cook, a milliner, and many others. The cook, Oswald Medcalfe, was so angry at being evicted he protested Charles's decree to the Council of State. Medcalfe argued that he had rented his house on a multiyear contract and that cooks had used the house for forty years. Further, while some goldsmiths had looked at the house, they all said that it was too dark and so "unfit for goldsmiths." Since neither the goldsmiths nor the landlord would take it from him, Medcalfe asked that he be allowed to keep his shop.[31] His landlord supported his report by saying that "my intent . . . was . . . that the [shop] may be let to a goldsmith, but . . . it has been refused by many goldsmiths . . . through the darkness thereof and the narrowness of the street."[32]

While existing tenants were a problem, there were also goldsmiths who could not move because they could not afford it. Goldsmith Thomas Crosse petitioned the Lord Mayor of London nearly every day in May and June 1635 for a reprieve from the king's edict. Crosse argued that he could not relocate because his wife and family would face calamitous financial ruin if he was forced to move.[33] Crosse's predicament may have encouraged his fellow goldsmiths to take a stand against the king's orders. In July 1635, contending that it would be catastrophically bad for their trade, forty-nine goldsmiths refused to move to Cheapside and Lombard Streets. Their strategy worked. Three years later, the Crown's agents were still menacing the goldsmiths who had not moved, but these were sounding more and more like what they were—empty threats.[34]

Charles made several mistakes in his dealings with the Goldsmiths' Company. First, using only coercion to try to change their behavior, he destroyed any goodwill that members may have had for him. Then, he had not investigated to discover if the goldsmiths had the space or financial wherewithal to move to Cheapside and Lombard Streets before he gave the order. Since his demands were impossible to meet, the goldsmiths had compelling arguments for flouting his command. Once they ignored him in this matter, though, his authority came into question. Adding to the goldsmiths' growing disdain, Charles appeared weak as his government wasted time listening to appeals by cooks like Oswald Medcalfe and ignoring their pleas. His uninformed rash decisions ultimately left him worse off than he had been before. He did not end corruption among the goldsmiths—the whole point of the operation—and he lost their respect.

By the middle of 1635, even though he was not willing to retreat, Charles and his advisors knew that they were not going to successfully relocate all of London's goldsmiths to Cheapside and Lombard Streets. At this time they may have stumbled onto another solution of controlling their goldsmiths; they could use Thomas Violet to inform on the goldsmiths who were illegally exporting money out of the country. Violet had already shown his loyalty to the government. After all, he had not only betrayed his confederates but also paid a £2,000 fine for his own role in illegal currency exchanges. In addition, Violet was not simply a caught and repentant sinner, he was also a competent one. When he traded Henry Flutter's light gold for French silver, Violet had actually made money for the kingdom of England. The English government even had irrefutable evidence to prove Violet's value: Violet's troubles had exposed his business partners in France, causing the French government to launch an investigation of its own into their activities. Quickly, Violet's French counterparts were brought before the Parliament of Paris (the major French court) on charges that they undersold French silver to an English merchant! When Secretary Coke confirmed this tidbit of news, he had to have smiled. Thomas Violet had swindled the French out of a small fortune, humiliated them, and brought a sizable amount of money to his king. Such a man could be very useful.[35]

Some time after Violet recovered from his illness, King Charles and Secretary Coke spoke about Violet at length. They realized that Violet had a very specific skill set that could be incredibly valuable. First, he clearly understood money and how to make it. Second, he obviously was closely connected to virtually everyone who worked in gold and silver in London and with many merchants who bought and sold coins overseas. As his widespread trade from 1632 to 1634 had shown, he was industrious, ambitious, competent, and sneaky. He was also an immigrants' son and so did not have family connections with the official body that oversaw gold production in London. He was a perfect candidate for the position Charles wanted filled: a spy among the goldsmiths. Charles had found the one man who could help him regulate all aspects of the goldsmiths' business activities. If he had someone on the inside who could tell him what they were doing illegally, someone who had great knowledge of the trade, it could provide both a political and an economic boon to the king. Charles would more efficiently control the rare metals in his kingdom and the fines he would collect from his miscreant goldsmiths would help pay for his government.

Coke made the offer to Violet. Violet accepted. He was now not just a goldsmith but also a government spy.[36]

NOTES

1. Sir Henry St. George, *The Visitation of London, Anno Domini 1633, 1634, 1635*, ed. Joseph Jackson Howard (London: Harleian Society, 1883), 314; PROB 20/2650; Anon., *The Great Trappanner of England Discovered* (London, 1660), 1; Ariel Hessayon, "'The Great Trappaner of England': Thomas Violet, Jews and Crypto-Jews during the English Revolution and at the Restoration," in *The Experience of Revolution in Stuart Britain and Ireland*, eds. Michael J. Braddick and David L. Smith (Cambridge: Cambridge University Press, 2011), 213; Samuel Pepys, *The Diary of Samuel Pepys: A Selection*, ed. Robert Latham (London: Penguin Books, 1985), 1040–41. Peter and Sara Vyolett were buried in St. Katharine Creechurch, so it is likely they lived in the parish. See PROB 20/2650.

2. See Walter Prideaux, *Memorials of the Goldsmiths' Company* (London: Worshipful Company of Goldsmiths, 1896), ix–xxviii, for a summary of the Goldsmiths' Company.

3. St. George, *The Visitation of London, Anno Domini 1633, 1634, 1635*, 257; Hessayon, "'The Great Trappaner of England,'" 213.

4. See *Calendar of State Papers Domestic (CSPD), 1633–34*, 576, for how his name is spelled in 1634. The Goldsmiths' Company always remembered where he came from, though, spelling his name "Vyolett" through the 1630s. Prideaux, *Memorials of the Goldsmiths' Company*, 174.

5. See C. E. Challis, "Lord Hastings to the Great Silver Recoinage, 1464–1699," in *A New History of the Royal Mint*, ed. C. E. Challis (Cambridge: Cambridge University Press, 1992), 310, for the value of gold in 1625.

6. John Rushworth, *Historical Collections*, vol. 2 (London: n.p., 1721), 351; PROB 20/2650.

7. Mark Kishlansky, *A Monarchy Transformed: Britain 1603–1714* (London: Penguin Books, 1996), 121.

8. Rushworth, *Historical Collections*, vol. 2, 351.

9. Ibid., 350.

10. The sum of £1,000 was a fortune. If Violet had earned that much a year, he would have been among the top 2 percent of English society. See Robert Bucholz and Newton Key, *Early Modern England 1485–1714*, 2nd ed. (Singapore: Wiley-Blackwell, 2009), 161.

11. Rushworth, *Historical Collections*, vol. 2, 351.

12. "Cardecu," *Oxford English Dictionary*, Second Edition, vol. 2 (Oxford: Oxford University Press, 1989), 890.

13. Thomas Violet, *The Advancement of Merchandize* (London, [17 Feb.] 1651), 101.

14. Rushworth, *Historical Collections*, vol. 2, 351; Challis, "Lord Hastings to the Great Silver Recoinage, 1464–1699," 318; Hessayon, "'The Great Trappaner of England,'" 213.

15. Prideaux, *Memorials of the Goldsmiths' Company*, 155, 161.

16. Elizabeth Glover, *The Gold & Silver Wyre-Drawers* (London: Phillimore, 1979), 6, 10.

17. Violet, *The Advancement of Merchandize*, 98–100.

18. *CSPD, 1633–34*, 495; Violet, *The Advancement of Merchandize*, 98.

19. Susan Brigden, *New Worlds, Lost Worlds: The Rule of the Tudors* (London: Penguin Books, 2000), 165.

20. Lacey Baldwin Smith, *This Realm of England 1399–1688*, 8th ed. (New York: Houghton Mifflin, 2001), 101, 275–76.

21. Violet, *The Advancement of Merchandize*, 99–100.

22. Ibid., 99–101; *CSPD, 1633–34*, 576.

23. Violet, *The Advancement of Merchandize*, 100–102; *CSPD, 1633–34*, 576.

24. PROB 20/2650.

25. Prideaux, *Memorials of the Goldsmiths' Company*, 155; PROB 20/2650, first document, second and third pages.

26. *CSPD, 1633–34*, 495.

27. Prideaux, *Memorials of the Goldsmiths' Company*, 64, 65.

28. Ibid., 49, 51.

29. *CSPD, 1634–35*, 288; paragraph continues onto 289.

30. *CSPD, 1637–38*, 155.

31. Ibid., 272–73.

32. Ibid., 330–31.

33. *CSPD, 1635*, 79, 167.

34. Ibid., 237–38; *CSPD, 1637*, 145.

35. Violet, *The Advancement of Merchandize*, 101–2; *CSPD, 1633–34*, 576.

36. Violet, *The Advancement of Merchandize*, 102–3; *CSPD, 1636–37*, 267, 402, for the first examples of Violet's spy work. For a different chronology of these years, see Hessayon, "'The Great Trappaner of England,'" 213–14.

Chapter Two

Spy

From 1635 to 1640, Violet embarked on a new career. Instead of trying to make money by avoiding the law, he would earn it by enforcing the king's regulations. He knew that his fellow goldsmiths would hate him because he was going to spy on them for the government, but after his recovery from his suicide attempt he believed espionage was his only viable option. During these years, he pursued several duplicitous avenues to earn steady revenue for the king. Initially, Violet strove to capture goldsmiths who were illegally exporting gold. In this endeavor, Violet worked closely with two of Charles's most important ministers: the senior secretary of state, Sir John Coke, and Sir John Bankes, the attorney general. Both wanted Violet to use his knowledge of the goldsmith trade to raise money for the Crown.[1] Bankes and Coke instructed Violet that he had to demonstrate incontestable proof of the goldsmiths' corruption. If he did so, the government would reimburse him all the expenses he incurred during his investigation as well as reward him in other ways. Assuming he would earn a fortune, Violet followed Coke's and Bankes's orders enthusiastically.

Violet used all of his contacts to bring down the goldsmiths. For almost two years, he paid informants in England and on the continent to collect evidence against them. Violet's spies acquired the goldsmiths' business letters, which revealed the extent of their illegal behavior. The letters were written in code. Violet's men demonstrated that if a goldsmith mentioned exporting "needles, Blades, Glovers, Ribbon, [and] roles of Tobacco," it meant that he was illegally exporting gold. Violet's agents then contacted the French merchants with whom the English goldsmiths conducted their business and bribed these Frenchmen to come to England and testify before Attorney General Bankes. Due to Violet's efforts, the government gained undeniable proof that the goldsmiths were guilty, allowing Bankes to bring charges against sixteen of them. [2]

Since the whole point of Violet's work was to raise revenue for the government, instead of imprisoning the offenders, King Charles's ministers fined them. Fines ranged from £500 to an astronomically high £4,000. Among the men on Violet's list were his old business partner Henry Flutter, who owed £500 and his former master, Timothy Eman, charged £2,000. When all the fines were tallied, the fourteen goldsmiths who were found guilty owed the government £24,100. This enormous sum equaled nearly two and a half percent of the government's annual revenue. Only two goldsmiths avoided any legal charges: the rich and powerful John Wollaston and William Gibs, future and present, respectively, Aldermen of the City of London. Being an Alderman secured each a seat on the governing board of the City of London. These two politically connected men managed to get King Charles to drop the charges against them, perhaps by giving the king a substantial amount of money. [3]

Violet's efforts managed to net the government sizable revenue, and he expected his share of the profits. He spent £1,968 of his own money in the nearly two-year-long operation of paying people to investigate the goldsmiths and bringing foreigners to England to testify against them. Understandably, he wanted the government to reimburse him, but Bankes and Coke never authorized any payments to Violet. Charles's government needed every penny, and the secretary of state and attorney general most likely did not want to lose a small fortune to Thomas Violet. Infuriated, Violet constantly demanded the government make good on what it owed him. While he continued to lobby Bankes and Coke for his money, Violet realized that if the Council of State granted him a regulatory post, he would more than earn back his £1,968. The question was—what type of position could he convince the Crown's officers to hire him to do? With his enormous ego and unabashed greed, he set his sight on nothing less than being made overseer for all gold and silver production in London. [4]

Violet laid the groundwork for this plot in the winter of 1636–37. During that time he communicated with Henry Rich, the Earl of Holland. (English aristocrats have a name, but also a title. The title is often not their family name. So Henry Rich's title was Earl of Holland. Contemporaries would have referred to him by his title.) The Earl of Holland was an astute choice for Violet to cultivate. Holland was incredibly rich, earning £10,000–13,000 a year, an income that placed him among the ten wealthiest men in England. He was about as politically connected as anyone could be; a personal friend and intimate of both King Charles and Queen Henrietta-Maria, he spent large amounts of time with both monarchs. He held numerous elite government positions. Yet, he wanted even more power and money.[5] As avaricious as Violet, Holland was a perfect ally in the attempt to take control of all of England's bullion.

Their plan was brilliant in conception. The government would set up an "Exchange." All of the gold in the kingdom, before it was manufactured into plate, coins, or anything else, would have to go through the Exchange. There, it would be tested for quality. If it passed muster, a government employee would stamp it, marking it fit to be sold. This process would standardize the value of gold used in England. While ensuring the quality of gold in England was important for the economy, the government directly benefited from this scheme because it would receive one penny for every ounce of gold that the Exchange processed. The best part of the plan was that it would use an existing organization to do all of the work—the Goldsmiths' Company. The goldsmiths had just finished building a new hall in 1636 and it could be utilized as the clearinghouse for the kingdom's wealth. Further, the goldsmiths' specialized skills allowed them to determine the quality of the gold that they gave the king's stamp. Finally, because they were in the heart of London, it would be very easy for the government to oversee the process. Of course, it would not be "the government" that oversaw the operations but, rather, the king's agents. In this case, the agent would be Thomas Violet.

Setting up the Exchange was not a new idea. In fact, in 1627 Holland had managed to convince the king that he deserved "the Great Seal of the office of Exchanger." Charles tried to revive this medieval office that had long been vacant in order to take over the gold trade. Holland's first gambit mirrored Violet's endeavor in that it attempted to channel all the gold in the king's realms into one clearinghouse. However, in 1627 the Goldsmiths' Company had violently resisted the notion because it would "bring utter destruction to more than 1,000 families" by hampering their trade.[6] The king dropped the idea, probably because of other political problems in 1627, but it remained in the public discourse. The plan only needed someone to revive it. Violet no doubt told the Earl of Holland that it was now time to act, sure that his specialized knowledge of the gold trade would help make the plan come to fruition.

Holland brought the new plan to the king and soon had King Charles and the attorney general of England (probably Sir John Bankes) completely behind the scheme.[7] The attorney general worked out the details of the Exchange with Holland and Violet. The only errand left was to inform the Goldsmiths' Company and see when it could begin implementing the scheme. In February 1637 Holland sent Violet to a meeting of the Court of Assistants (the governing body) of the Goldsmiths' Company to introduce the plan to the goldsmiths.[8]

Violet had wisely avoided the Goldsmiths' Hall once he had begun prosecuting goldsmiths for the government. Before approaching individual members with his plan, he had to first make peace with the company. Therefore, during the February 8, 1637, meeting of the Court of Assistants, Violet publicly apologized to the Goldsmiths' Company. The minutes of the meeting show that he repented for having "accused divers [i.e., various] person[s] of transportation of gold and silver, on the ground, that, his own life being in question, he was compelled to do what he had done; but now that he has obtained his pardon, he is endeavoring to do the Company a service." Violet explained that he had been meeting with the Council of State and the attorney general. They had told him that the government wanted to levy some sort of fine on the Goldsmiths' Company. Violet defended the company to Attorney General Bankes by attesting that it could not afford to contribute anything extra to the government at the moment, because it had spent so much money on the new hall and some bad investments in Irish property. Further, Violet informed the goldsmiths that, in his conversations with Bankes and the Council of State, he had insinuated that individual members were as poor as they had ever been, due to the decline in their trade over the last twenty years. Violet assured the Court of Assistants that his comments to the council were sufficient to prevent it from extracting money from the company.

Having laid the groundwork for a truce between himself and the goldsmiths, Violet then proceeded to outline his and Holland's new scheme for the Exchange. He explained that Attorney General Bankes had empowered him to negotiate with the Goldsmiths' Company all of the details about how the Exchange would work. He informed them that the Goldsmiths' Hall would now be the clearinghouse of all the gold in England and that they would be reporting directly to him from now on. Violet also told the goldsmiths that they should proceed immediately and begin preparing the hall for its new role in the English economy. Violet concluded by demanding that the goldsmiths report their progress to him before the next Council of State meeting.

The plan appalled the Goldsmiths' Company and immediately provoked objections. The membership saw several problems. The first and most obvious was that they did not want to be under Violet's thumb. If the entirety of the gold in the kingdom was to pass through their halls and be supervised by Violet, he would control all of them because he could, at any time, charge any of them with tampering with the nation's money supply. As the company pointed out to the Council of State a few weeks later, "it is very inconvenient that the monies and treasures of England, Wales, and Ireland must . . . come into the hands of one subject." If the government went forward with the Exchange, it meant the end of a free Goldsmiths' Company and the beginnings of a government department overseen by a scoundrel.[9]

The second issue, which the goldsmiths gleefully announced to the Council of State, was the plan's impracticality. If the members of the Exchange sold the gold they collected to men making plate or other decorative pieces for a higher price than the mint could pay, then the Exchange would shortchange the mint. Since the mint relied on a steady supply of gold and silver to produce coins, the kingdom would soon face a currency shortage. No one could defend the mint either because it would be controlled by the Exchange.

The goldsmiths' final argument emphasized the importance of free trade to their work. They wrote, "It is a great discouragement to the merchant to import bullion to vend to the mint with great trouble or loss, or else to the Exchange at less value than a goldsmith would give with a free market." The Goldsmiths' Company suggested that a free market, or the free trade of goods, ensured the best possible price for everyone. Merchants were much better off selling their gold to the goldsmiths, who often acted like bankers, than taking the government's below-market price for their product. In conclusion the goldsmiths asserted that government regulation of their business would actually strangle it and destroy them while at the same time hurt the nation's money supply.[10]

The Goldsmiths' Company's concerns effectively halted Violet's plan. By February 21, Violet publicly denied that he had attended the Court of Assistants meeting on February 8 in order to shield himself from the political storm that ensued his initial presentation. When King Charles and Coke learned that the Goldsmiths' Company was not keen on setting up the Exchange, as Holland and Violet had led them to believe, Violet's first instinct was to lie to the earl and deny attending the company meeting in order to protect himself from the repercussions of causing a political tempest. This only delayed the inevitable, however, and by March 17, Violet's plan had collapsed. That day, Attorney General Bankes and the Goldsmiths' Company's representatives convinced Secretary of State John Coke that not only would government regulation destroy the goldsmiths, but that only a free market would maintain England's gold supply. By all accounts, Coke was the king's best administrator in England in the late 1630s. He was a man who actually understood how the government and economy interacted. If he could be convinced by the idea that free trade was a more effective way of organizing an economy than a government monopoly, then free trade indeed had powerful supporters. (The issue of free trade will be explored more fully in chapter 4.) The result was that the Goldsmiths' Company saved itself by arguing that it was in the nation's interest to avoid the Exchange and instead allow the market to work unimpeded.[11] Ultimately, Violet's grand plan for the goldsmiths did not succeed because too many powerful men opposed it.

Undaunted by his failure, he realized that if he wanted to regulate some aspect of gold and silver production in England, he needed to pick a weaker target. So he zeroed in on a smaller prize, one that he had been working on for several years: the overseeing of the gold and silver wire drawers. In this case he found success. Violet investigated them, provided evidence that they were hurting the balance of trade, and King Charles rewarded him with a position that gave him the power to regulate and fine them.

Many differences separated the goldsmiths and the gold and silver wire drawers. Not only were the goldsmiths wealthier, they also had their own company, which allowed them, among other things, to present a united front to the government on matters that impacted them. The much poorer gold and silver wire drawers realized that they could increase their political clout by incorporating themselves. In March 1634 and again in April 1635, the wire drawers had petitioned the "King for a Corporation."[12] The wire drawers suggested to the government that their corporation pay the king £1,000 a year for the privilege of a charter. Further, they would compensate the government two pence for every ounce of bullion they used to produce their gold and silver thread. The wire drawers ensured that the government knew how much gold and silver they used because it would all be funneled through "one or two Refiners." Refiners melted down plate and coinage to make the gold and silver ingots that wire drawers used as a base material. The men who laid out this proposal to the government were the wire drawers, and brothers, Joseph and William Symonds.[13]

The Symonds brothers faced resistance from the Goldsmiths' Company, who attempted to prevent them from forming their own corporation. Goldsmith John Wollaston led the fight against the wire drawers. He was a refiner as well as a goldsmith. Wollaston, along with seven other goldsmiths, had already negotiated a deal with the government giving them the monopoly on refining all the gold and silver that the wire drawers could legally purchase and they did not want to lose control of their lucrative trade. They rightly feared that the wire drawers would use one of their own as a refiner, rather than relying on a goldsmith. To prevent this from happening, the eight refiners of London bribed the government to forbid the gold and silver wire drawers from forming their own company.[14]

Under lobbying from both groups, the government compromised. It laid out rules and regulations, allegedly requested by the wire drawers, yet these same decrees prevented them from establishing their own corporation. The government conceived a five-point plan. The first was that the wire drawers only use foreign gold and silver to produce their wire. Second, these precious metals could not be purchased with English currency but rather had to be traded for with English goods. If they followed points one and two, then the third point applied: there would be no restrictions as to how much gold and silver they imported. The fourth point asserted that whatever they manufactured had to "be made according to the Standard, [i.e., the government requirement for gold to be of a certain quality] or better." And the fifth point said that they could not raise the price of their commodities.[15]

While these discussions were going on, Thomas Violet conducted a lengthy investigation of the wire drawers that hinted that they were defrauding the realm. Once he presented this information to King Charles in 1635, Charles ordered Violet and a few other men "to search . . . several Shops in London." During this raid of the gold and silver wire drawers' properties, Violet found "one hundred and odde several parcels of course and adulterate wire, thread, lace, and spangles." All of these goods, including the spangles, were "exposed and bended for goods silver." Violet had proof that the wire drawers were selling goods they claimed to be pure but in fact were cut with lesser metals, thus defrauding customers.[16]

After these searches, Violet decided it was time to show the government what he could do for it if he had a regular position overseeing the wire drawers. In January 1636, Violet drew up a contract with the government that would grant him the authority to police the gold and silver wire trade. Violet told the king that he believed a well-regulated trade among the gold and silver wire drawers would net the government up to £8,000 a year. This enormous sum could be reached, Violet claimed, if every single bit of gold and silver that the wire drawers could process had to be stamped by a king's official. Putting his own name forward, Violet explained he had the where-withal to stamp every ingot that the refiners produced for gold and silver wire drawers' use as well as providing a written receipt for them. During this process, Violet would make sure that the gold and silver wire drawers were using the appropriate quality of gold and silver. While he gave different estimates on how much money this would yield the government, the most frequent figure he cited was ten shillings for every hundred pounds of stamped gold and silver, or about £8,000 a year in fines.[17]

Although impressed with Violet's work, Charles did not immediately reward him with a position. No doubt part of the reason for the delay was Violet's disastrous attempts in 1636–37 to regulate gold production in London. It was not until the early fall of 1638 that Charles agreed to Violet's idea. Charles finally granted Violet's petition for several reasons. First, Charles believed that he was getting someone who could improve the quality of gold and silver thread in England. Second, the king felt he owed Violet for the £1,968 that Violet spent prosecuting the goldsmiths in 1635–37 and wanted to reward him without paying him any money. Third, in the fall of 1638 the king himself desperately needed money and his advisors hoped that Thomas Violet would be an industrious overseer of the gold and silver wire drawers. They believed he would fine them so much that he would bring in a steady stream of revenue for the government. All three factors combined in Violet's favor and on September 7, 1638, King Charles I gave Thomas Violet the right to oversee "all these Manufactures" of "Gold or Silver Thread."[18]

Charles had such high expectations for Violet's operation that he author-ized a four-man team to help Violet oversee the wire drawers. Considering that there were only thirty wire drawers in London, Charles wanted every bit of the promised £8,000 a year in fines. Violet's employees each had their own role. Francis Archer was his clerk. Archer recorded all the transactions with the gold and silver wire drawers. Andrew Palmer, the assay master of the mint, determined the quality of their product and drew a £50 a year salary for his trouble. Meanwhile, Violet assigned Leonard Welsted the role of comptroller and keeper of the "Counter accounts," which means he would do the double-entry bookkeeping. Finally, Robert Amery was his messenger.[19] Violet expected to interview the wire drawers and hunt down those his team found in violation of the regulations. Violet did not enjoy the first part of his job because the gold and silver wire drawers were almost never happy to go to his place of business to be certified. He complained that "it is no small trouble to have daily conversation with people of such several humors, and some of them of such uncivil and coarse behavior that" he thought no one had heard the like. He felt that the wire drawers "must needs bee clamorous when the officer [meaning Violet] doth his duty to see they make all good work."[20] Of course, the reason the men might have been in such an "uncivil and coarse" mood was that, by Violet's own reckoning, during the four years he oversaw them he and his men found "above one hundred several affairs" where the wire drawers were using "coarse and adulterated" gold and silver.[21] With thirty gold and silver wire drawers in the city, it is likely that he and his team fined every wire drawer in the city three or four times. No wonder they hated him.

One reason Violet's men worked so hard was that they were paid on commission. Violet's original deal with the king was that he would earn four pennies for every pound of gold and silver he stamped.[22] At this time, English currency was divided into pounds, shillings, and pence (penny). A shilling was worth twelve pennies and a pound was worth twenty shillings or two hundred and forty pennies. Four pence a pound then was not much revenue. The consequence of this contract was that Violet's pay depended on volume and that if he wanted a significant and regular income he needed to fine as many people as possible.

He started by attacking the Symonds brothers. Joseph and William Symonds had been the driving force behind the effort in 1634 and 1635 to create a Gold and Silver Wire Drawers' Company. Violet knew that if, for some reason, they managed to actually convince the king to give them a charter, he would be out of a potentially lucrative position, and for this reason he decided to destroy them. To do this, he had to break their reputations and prove to the king's government that they were routinely violating the king's laws. After he became the overseer of the gold and silver wire drawers, but before they knew what kind of overseer he would be, Violet spent time socializing with the Symonds brothers and their fellow wire drawers George Pickering and Richard Gibbs. Since he had worked with wire drawers from 1632 to 1634, Violet may have even been renewing old acquaintances. They were comfortable enough around each other to joke and swap amusing stories. During their conversations in the fall of 1638, Violet shared comical stories about his own business practices. Violet talked openly and with a wry humor about how he smuggled bullion and had been found out by the government and fined. No doubt he recalled particular episodes to Joseph and William and described how he cheated the French or the English authorities. Once he had shared his stories with them, they started opening up to him. As gold and silver wire drawers, they had scores of stories to tell about how they had destroyed precious metals, defrauded customers, and cheated the government of tax revenue. Almost certainly, when Violet was holding these conversations with the Symonds brothers, Pickering, and Gibbs, he prevented his office from bearing down on them too hard, so they would start to feel that he could be trusted. Violet probably took them out together as a group to a tavern where he paid for the drinks. [23]

However, when he thought he had enough evidence against his drinking companions, Violet pounced. On November 15, 1638, he presented a petition to the Council of State alleging that Joseph and William Symonds, as well as George Pickering and Richard Gibbs, had made "Scandalous speeches" that revealed they had defrauded the government. They were arrested, incarcerated, and forbidden to "buy or sell any gold or silver . . . to their great damage." On November 29 they offered a counterpetition to the Council of State. [24] Two weeks later the council brought in the four men for questioning. When they heard the charges against them and they learned that Violet had brought the accusations, they were stunned. As the members of the council read out excerpts from various conversations that they had taken part in over recent months, they claimed "that they do not remember that they uttered such speeches." Of course they acknowledged that they had spoken to Thomas Violet the previous month and that there were "speeches of variance," meaning that they had spoken to him about a great many topics. However, if they claimed to have done anything illegal, it was only "in a jesting manner." [25]

What happened next is not clear from the records left in the Council of State. William Symonds, George Pickering, and Richard Gibbs were all set free because there was "no proof . . . against [them] . . . besides Violet's affidavit." [26] Further, the council thought that these three men "may be useful for his Majesty's services, and having engaged themselves to be for the future conformable to government, we conceive . . . to free them, and restore their liberty." [27] While William Symonds, Pickering, and Gibbs all got off with a warning, Joseph Symonds had more trouble. He faced charges brought "by the affidavit of three witnesses." The Council of State never identified the witnesses, but it might not be too much of a coincidence that it freed three men and three men testified against Joseph. If these two sets of three men were in fact the same people, then William Symonds threw his brother to the wolves and blamed him for their respective crimes. William may have done this because Joseph could cry poverty in front of the council and beg for mercy for the sake of his children. The council found Joseph to be repentant, and urged the king to be forgiving. If all this occurred, as seems likely, Violet had not only humiliated the wire drawers, he had also divided them.[28]

Having divided them in December 1638, in February 1640 Violet went in for the kill. The brothers' silver supplier, William Green, sold them silver that Violet had not stamped. In order to shield it from Violet, the brothers hid the silver in a friend's house. Violet's men, no doubt watching the Symonds family closely, caught wind of their plan. Violet sent Robert Amery to the house where they had hid the silver. There, Amery fought the residents for the silver. It was well worth the struggle. Amery found "two bars of silver and one of silver gilt," which were worth £170.[29] Since the Symonds brothers had tried to hide the silver from Violet, they lost it all. Violet's actions shattered the Symonds brothers' business. They never recovered and ten years later, Joseph Symonds's widow still blamed Violet for ruining her family.[30]

Violet attacked the wire drawers not only in the production process but also in the wholesale part of their business. In fact, the easiest way for Violet and his team to catch delinquents was to prove that the gold and silver wire drawers had sold wire with a copper core. They would cover the copper core with gold or silver and thus sell the wire at artificially high prices. When he found out that a wire drawer named Gares had done just that, Violet proudly announced, "I caused Gares to stand him the Pillory."[31]

While small-time operators like Gares could be humiliated, they did not turn much profit. Violet aimed much higher when he investigated Edward Bradbourn, Queen Henrietta-Maria's wire drawer, for fraud. The queen held extravagant dances, called masques, which virtually all the aristocrats in the country attended. The queen required attendees to wear elaborate costumes often decorated with vast amounts of gold and silver thread.[32] Bradbourn had the great fortune to be the queen's supplier of gold and silver thread and it is little wonder that he had many aristocratic clients. For the masque of 1637, his shop produced 2,000 ounces of gold and silver lace. During the production of this vast quantity of fine gold and silver wire, several of Bradbourn's apprentices made some mistakes. These were small errors but two nobles, an unnamed "noble lady" and Lord Carlisle, bought silver thread that had some copper mixed in it. Lord Carlisle was furious that he had walked around with a "Suit and Cloak" made up of copper. Violet never explains, nor do the government records indicate, at what stage in the production process Violet discovered this. However, it almost certainly happened after he was appointed to oversee the gold and silver wire drawers in 1638. His plan emulated his Symonds brothers scheme: by destroying Bradbourn's reputation, and hence damaging his business, he would be able to fine him.[33]

Violet's accusations that Bradbourn used copper to make his gold and silver thread reached the ears of both the aristocratic consumers of the goods and the other gold and silver drawers. Even if Violet did not have any proof that Bradbourn was acting illegally, his allegations hurt Bradbourn's reputation among the aristocrats and hence his business. Bradbourn forcefully acted to counter the allegations. He admitted that his servants had made a mistake in the incredibly large order of 2,000 ounces of refined gold and silver that Queen Henrietta-Maria demanded. This tiny mistake occurred on only two ounces, he claimed. Further, once Bradbourn learned of the error, he contacted the two nobles and offered to replace the copper thread with gold. All of this did not completely clear his name, though, and, in fact, by 1639 Violet felt that he had softened up Bradbourn's reputation enough to bring charges against him.[34]

On July 26, 1639, the Council of State heard Violet's allegations against Edward Bradbourn and Bradbourn's defense. While weighing the evidence, the Earl of Dorset told the council that the queen "was pleased to take knowledge of Bradbourn's well deserving in her service." Further, she wanted the council to know of his "fair and honest dealing in his trade" and that "the scandal [caused by the] . . . occasion of the complaint" had hurt the good man's business.[35] After Dorset delivered the queen's message to the council, it quickly found him innocent "notwithstanding a petition of Thomas Violet to have the business further heard by the board." Then Queen Henrietta-Maria sent Violet a message that explicitly commanded him to let the matter drop.[36] In this case, Violet had overreached. He angered the queen and had to halt the investigation.

Violet may have overplayed his hand in his investigation of Bradbourn because 1638 was the best year of his life. He had made himself useful to the king and earned the king's Exchequer tens of thousands of pounds in fines. His office of overseeing the gold and silver wire drawers earned him £300 a year. He also became the tax collector responsible for collecting one quarter of the taxes levied on imported gold and silver used to make the gold and silver thread. This post earned him £150 a year. Then, in an incredible move, he became a member of the landed gentry.[37]

The landed gentry defined social success in early modern England. To be a member of this elite group, a man had to own enough land to generate sufficient revenue for him to live on the income from it. Owning a large estate was the ultimate goal of any wealthy tradesman or professional. By doing so, a man could ensure that his children would join the highest status group—the gentlemen—in English society. Men acquired enough land to join the gentry in a variety of ways, including purchasing it or inheriting it, or sometimes the king rewarded followers with estates. Another way to procure land was to take advantage of someone else's bankruptcy, which is what Violet did.

Violet seized two manors in the summer of 1638. Two brothers-in-law, Philip Cage and Charles Mordant, faced terrible financial difficulties. Their problems stemmed from mistakes that they made investing in the Silk Office, the government body that regulated silk production and tax collection. In early modern England, the Crown sold the rights to collect the taxes on particular goods to individuals. These men were called "tax farmers." A tax farmer would pay for a particular position and then be responsible for collecting taxes on that product for the rest of his life. Charles Mordant was part of an investment team that paid £2,000 to collect taxes for the Silk Office. The key to being a successful tax farmer was to collect more taxes from the people than the government expected. Once the tax farmer paid the government its money, he could pocket all the rest of the taxes he collected that year, which allowed the tax farmers to recover their investment and earn money.

Violet did this; he owned one quarter of the tax farm on the import of gold and silver that would be turned into thread. Unlike Violet, Charles Mordant was not a very good tax farmer. He and his brother-in-law Philip Cage barely collected enough money to pay their obligation to the government. Since they needed the tax money to pay for their lavish lifestyles, their inability to collect taxes spelled financial ruin. By the summer of 1638, the two men could not pay their bills and were about to go bankrupt. In order to save their manors, on July 8, 1638, they came to an agreement with Violet.[38]

The two men owned a fair amount of land. The choice bits were in the county of Essex where there were two small manors, named Battles Hall and Patton Hall. They also owned rental property in London. In return for a £3,000 loan, the Cage and Mordant families gave up their properties to Violet. He estimated their value at £11,000. He could live there and collect the rents from the properties while the men tried to earn their way out of debt.[39] Violet assumed Mordant and Cage would never redeem their properties, because they were so incompetent they could not even make money by farming the silk tax. For only £3,000 Violet had just purchased the life of a gentleman. Only four years after he was imprisoned by the government, he was now the proud owner of not one, but two manors. He was by any definition a success.

Spying on his fellows, earning their enduring hatred, reporting their activities to the king, and threatening and exposing gold and silver wire drawers—all of these activities had made Violet rich. It appears that God was right and that Violet had survived his 1634 suicide attempt for a good reason. Clearly, helping the government spy and regulate the gold trade meant that the future was bright and full of money. It is little wonder Violet felt confident enough to go after the queen's gold and silver wire drawer. Everything else had worked out so well. Violet could reasonably believe that nothing could dim his prospects as long as the political system on which he based his accomplishments did not collapse. There was little worry about that, however, because the country had been stable for the last century and a half, and no one could imagine it would descend into chaos again.

NOTES

1. Kevin Sharpe, *The Personal Rule of Charles I* (New Haven, CT: Yale University Press, 1992), 153–57, 257–59.

2. Thomas Violet, *An Humble Declaration to the Right Honourable the Lord and Commons in Parliament Assembled* (London, 1643), quote 4–5, 4–10. Violet says fourteen were charged on page 9 but explains on page 10 that two avoided the charges.

3. Ibid., 10–11.

4. Violet, *To the Kings Most Excellent Majesty* (London, 1662), 8; *CSPD, 1636–37*, 402.

5. Sharpe, *The Personal Rule of Charles I*, 164–65.

6. Prideaux, *Memorials of the Goldsmiths' Company*, 143.

7. Sharpe, *The Personal Rule of Charles I*, 257–59. For evidence that Violet knew Bankes, see Violet, *An Humble Declaration to the Right Honourable the Lord and Commons in Parliament Assembled*, 5.

8. Prideaux, *Memorials of the Goldsmiths' Company*, 174–75.

9. Ibid., 175–76.

10. Ibid., 176.

11. Ibid., 175–78.

12. Violet, *The Advancement of Merchandize*, 98.

13. Ibid., 98, 104, 107.

14. Ibid., 106, and see 108 for the number of refiners in London.

15. Ibid., 105.

16. Violet, *To the Kings Most Excellent Majesty*, quote 2; 2–3.

17. *CSPD, 1635–36*, 169; Violet, *The Advancement of Merchandize*, 112, 113.

18. Violet, *Two Petitions of Thomas Violet* (London, 1661), 21.

19. *CSPD, 1639–40*, 416 for Amery's name.

20. Violet, *The Advancement of Merchandize*, 112; *CSPD, 1635–36*, 169.

21. Violet, *The Advancement of Merchandize*, 110.

22. Ibid., 112.

23. *CSPD, 1638–39*, 171–72.

24. Ibid., 132.

25. Ibid., 171–72.

26. Ibid., 171.

27. Ibid., quote 171, 172.

28. Ibid.

29. *CSPD, 1639–40*, 416.

30. Violet, *The Advancement of Merchandize*, 122.

31. Ibid., 114.

32. See Sharpe, *The Personal Rule of Charles I*, 177n333.

33. *CSPD, 1639*, 419–20; Violet, *The Advancement of Merchandize*, 114.

34. *CSPD, 1639*, 419–20.

35. Ibid., 419.

36. Ibid., 419–20; Violet, *The Advancement of Merchandize*, 114.

37. Violet, *The Advancement of Merchandize*, 124–25.

38. *CSPD, 1625–49*, Addenda, 512.

39. Violet, *To the Right Honourable the Lords in Parliament Assembled* (London, 1660), 1; Violet, *The Advancement of Merchandize*, 125, 131–32.

Chapter Three

Royalist

Unfortunately for Violet, only a few years after his great triumph war broke out in England. Charles I and his Parliament quarreled about who controlled the political and religious destiny of the nation. By August 1642 the shooting had started. As for almost all men his age in England, Violet's actions during the war defined the rest of his life. The war separated the English along many fault lines: political, religious, cultural, financial, and personal. While Violet certainly had no religious or political motivations for choosing a side, his decision to become a Royalist developed out of multifaceted, interlocking circumstances. It required a combination of the king's efforts to debase the currency in 1640, the goldsmiths' reaction to the king, political developments in the city of London, and Parliament's tax laws to turn Violet from a neutral party in the conflict into a Royalist. Much to his consternation, the Royalists lost the war. Yet considering what he knew during the first two years of the war, it is hard to imagine that Violet would have made another choice because he based his allegiance on which side appeared to offer him a better opportunity to make money.

To better understand Violet's economic strategies, we need to place them in the context of the political and religious issues that scholars usually use to explain why the war started. In short, King Charles I wanted to force the three kingdoms he ruled, England, Scotland, and Ireland, to follow a nearly identical religion. His dream proved challenging to implement because most Irish were Catholics, most Scots were Presbyterians, and the English, while Protestant, were conflicted about the type of Protestant church they wanted the Church of England to be. Charles wanted them to follow Arminianism, which was a very Catholic, as opposed to Calvinist, type of the Protestant faith. When Charles tried to impose his religion on his Scottish subjects in 1637, they rebelled against him. Charles needed to raise an army to deal with his defiant Scottish subjects. He had a serious problem, though—he did not have any money to pay for his army.

Charles lacked the funds for an army because he could not work with Parliament. In English law, only Parliament could raise taxes. Charles, a terrible politician who demanded loyalty but rarely understood how to earn it, had disbanded his last Parliament in 1629 because they would not raise taxes to pay for his failed war with France. The next eleven-year period, from 1629 to 1640, when Charles governed without Parliament, historians call the Personal Rule.[1]

Even during these years, when he did not have to fight any wars, Charles was always desperate for money. When his attorney general told him that Thomas Violet could help him fine his unruly goldsmiths for illegally exporting gold and silver out of the country in 1635, he quickly seized the opportunity to use the devious goldsmith for his own ends. While penalizing illegal actions helped earn money, Charles also explored other options. He had his ministers look back at old laws passed in the Middle Ages to find any forgotten laws that were still legally binding that he could use to raise money. They found "fines associated with refusing a summons to be knighted, enclosure, hunting and building in royal forests, and the inheritance of widows and wards. In each case, violation of the law or use of a royal 'service' resulted in a fee to the Crown."[2] They also came up with a new scheme to tax the whole country for "Ship Money." In the Middle Ages, only the counties on the coast were taxed to help build a navy because everyone thought that they were the only ones who benefited from it. But Charles made the whole country pay this tax to fund his ships.

The ship money, the fines for illegal actions, and the other medieval laws helped ease the king's revenue problem. They did not, however, balance the budget. Charles only managed to do that because of a dramatic increase in customs revenue. During the 1630s all of Europe was at war except England, and English merchants managed to cut into Dutch and French merchants' trade. Expanded trade brought customs revenue to £358,000 in 1635, which was more than half of the government's total revenue.[3] By 1638 Charles's government managed to raise about £900,000 in revenue, which meant that the king was finally balancing his budget and not adding to the debt.[4]

The problem was, £900,000 a year did not begin to cover the cost of an army in 1639 to deal with the rebellious Scots. But Charles did not want to call Parliament to raise taxes to pay for the army because he did not trust it. When he went to war that year, it was the first time in centuries that an English monarch had taken the field without Parliament's support. Charles managed to build an army by relying on his aristocratic and gentry supporters to recruit from among their tenants. However, since English aristocrats had not fought in a war in 150 years and because they were not wealthy enough to equip their tenants, the result was that the force was poorly trained, poorly led, poorly armed, and dispirited as it marched north to Scotland in the summer of 1639. They were only held together by false promises and reluctant loyalty.

Meanwhile the Scots recruited their own army. Scotland's poor economy forced many Scots to go abroad as mercenaries to make a living. With their homeland threatened by foreign invasion, these professional soldiers came back to defend it. So Scotland was garrisoned by an army of experienced professionals, fighting to preserve the true faith, as they saw it, and the English were fighting for a king many did not respect. In fact, many English Puritans felt sympathy for the Scots. With so many problems, Charles did not risk a battle and instead in June 1639 reached a truce with the Scots that resolved nothing. Historians call this the First Bishops' War.

Since the Scots did not disband their army and had not accepted the king's religion, Charles decided to invade again. Yet by the spring of 1640 Charles could not afford to raise another army by himself. In the spring of 1640, he called for a Parliament that he hoped would raise taxes to fund an army to break Scottish resistance. However, the new Parliament would not grant funds for an army because it feared Charles would use his money to build an army, beat the Scots, and then crush English opposition to his political and religious reforms. Charles dissolved this Parliament after only three weeks, which gave it its name: "the Short Parliament." Things only got worse for Charles in the summer when his small army was defeated by the Scots' army, which occupied northern England (the Second Bishops' War). Having won the war, the Scots demanded £850 a day from the king to pay for their army. Now humiliated and out of options, the king had no choice but to call Parliament again. Parliament first met in November 1640 and did not finally dissolve itself until 1660—hence the name the "Long Parliament."

In the months from November 1640 to January 1642, the relationship between Charles and Parliament steadily worsened. The majority of the members of both the House of Commons and the House of Lords felt Charles had made mistakes in his political and religious decisions and that he needed to change course. Charles believed that no one could tell him what to do. When he was actually forced to do something, like sign the execution warrant for his chief lieutenant, the Earl of Strafford, for instance, he did so with poor grace and thinly disguised disgust. By the fall of 1641, Parliament had won most of the political battles because the king simply did not have much political support. Parliament at that point controlled the kingdom's political, religious, and fiscal future.

In the fall of 1641, however, something happened that changed the dynamic. The Irish rebelled. James I had planted many English and Scottish Protestant settlers in Ireland, taking land from Catholic Irish. In the fall of 1641, the Irish Catholics, seeing the confusion in London, attacked their Protestant overlords. It was a very bloody affair, with the Irish massacring the English and Scottish settlers. While these events were awful, when reported in England they were magnified tenfold. When news reached England in December 1641, English people were united in one cause—they had to raise an army to go kill the Irish Catholics and take revenge for the innocent Protestant women and children being raped, tortured, mutilated, and murdered.

Relations were so bad between the king and many in the House of Commons at this point, though, that the leaders of the House did not trust the king to do his constitutional duty. Although Parliament's role was to raise taxes, it was the king's responsibility to use the income to raise and lead an army. The leaders of the Commons feared that the king would use the army to kill not just Irish Catholics, but also parliamentary government in England. Not everyone in Parliament agreed with this interpretation, believing that the king should have the money to defend the kingdom. This split created the Royalist Party and the Roundhead Party. The Royalists thought that the king had a right to his army, but the Roundheads, so named because they were often Puritans and had shorter hair than the Royalists, disagreed. In January 1642 Charles fled London for Oxford after a botched attempt to capture his parliamentary opponents in the House of Commons. By August 1642, the two sides had gone to war.[5]

During the first three years of the English Civil War, the struggle followed a similar pattern. Parliament and the king would send out armies in the summer. They would fight at various locations throughout England. Sometimes Charles's forces would win and sometimes Parliament's troops triumphed. Through 1645, neither side gained a clear advantage. In the winter, they would negotiate because many men on both sides hated the war and wished it would stop. Too many people were dying and too much private property was being destroyed by the armies and taxation. While there were some aboveboard negotiations between Parliament and the king's agents, there were also many plots hatched by each side to undermine the other. Thus the first years of the English Civil Wars were unsettling. In the summer, everyone wondered how their armies were faring in the field, and in the winter, everyone pondered how their side was faring in the political maneuvering of the day.[6]

These plots and counterplots were perfectly suited for someone like Thomas Violet. Violet's actions during the first years of the English Civil War indicate that no matter what was going on around him, he was still true to the one thing he really believed in—to make more money for himself. It is not clear if Violet knew which side of the conflict he would support when the war started in 1642, but a series of decisions in the spring of 1643 drove him into the arms of the Royalists, where he set about plotting his way to greatness and unlimited riches. Like so many others, his path to Royalism was not straightforward. A series of actions by the king, Parliament, and the goldsmiths of London drove him to it.

Virtually all of the major goldsmiths in London supported Parliament during the war. They did so in no small part because they were more sympathetic to Parliament's religious goals but also because the king had tried to destroy their businesses. Charles had not intentionally attempted to bankrupt all of his goldsmiths and merchants but he had inadvertently almost done so in the summer of 1640. During those months, between the sitting of the Short Parliament and the Long Parliament, Charles was destitute. Scheming to pay for an army to fight the Scots, he made two decisions in July that permanently alienated his merchants from him.

On July 1, Charles had his ministers seize £130,000 of silver bullion held in the mint. This silver did not belong to Charles or his government. It was, in fact, Spanish silver being sent to the Netherlands. Because the Spanish and the Dutch were at war, merchants between the two countries could not openly trade. To avoid their own government's restrictions, Spanish merchants sent their gold to the English, who minted it into English coins, then transported them to the Netherlands where the Spanish bought goods with "English" coin, shipped the goods back to England, and then shipped them to Spain. This indirect trading was the key reason England had a healthy silver supply and why its merchants were prosperous. Now Charles threatened the whole enterprise. He promised to pay it back in six months, but everyone knew how low the royal coffers were and they did not believe that he would repay his loan. For the English merchants, Charles's order threatened them with ruin because the Spanish and the Dutch would realize that they could not trust their English counterparts to keep their money safe and so they might seek another broker.

If this was not bad enough, on July 11, Charles ordered the coinage to be debased. He decreed that a new copper coin be minted, with only one quarter its face value, which in effect created worthless English money.[7] The entire merchant community united against this travesty. Charles finally had to withdraw this idea, but his actions made it clear to the merchants and goldsmiths in London that Charles was prepared, even eager, to sacrifice their interests for his own. Consequently, with these two political errors, he made implacable enemies who supported Parliament both publicly and, perhaps even more important, financially.[8]

While the king had lost his goldsmiths' loyalty by the summer of 1640, he had yet to make Violet a Royalist partisan. Indeed, Violet was all over the map politically speaking in the years 1640–43. His testimony to Parliament on March 18, 1641, that he could prevent goldsmiths from transporting gold and silver out of the country illegally, indicated he supported Parliament, but this was before the king and Parliament irrevocably split.[9] Violet claims, but there is no other corroborating evidence, that he again testified before Parliament on April 12, 1643, regarding the same issue.[10] If Violet was telling the truth, then in the spring of 1643 he was willing to work with Parliament because he thought that he could have earned money by fining fellow goldsmiths just as he had done with the gold and silver wire drawers. Further, with Parliament desperate for bullion to pay for its troops and supplies, it is little wonder that men in the House of Commons would take his allegations—and his proposed solutions—seriously.

However, Violet failed to support Parliament in another very public way; he refused to pay his taxes. Like most Londoners, he felt the war most directly in 1642–43 by a dramatic increase in his tax rates. To finance its war effort, Parliament focused on three major sources of revenue. First, it began confiscating property owned by Royalists and selling the land for income. Then, it started collecting a national tax, called the Assessment. Imposed weekly, it forced every county under Parliament's control to pay a set amount of money. Finally, Parliament invented the excise tax, which modern economists call a sales tax. The excise brought in a fortune as it taxed highly desirable products like tobacco, beer, and ale. The result of these policies was that people paid between two and ten times as much in tax as they had under Charles in the 1630s—and that was when people complained about the tax rate! Further, they had to pay these new taxes at least weekly, if not daily. For someone who made his living by avoiding government regulations and fines, this was too much for Violet, and he chose not to pay these new taxes.[11]

Violet, though, had miscalculated because Sir John Wollaston was now the mayor of London. Wollaston was one of the London goldsmiths whom Violet had accused of illegally transporting gold out of the country in 1636. Wollaston was never formally charged because he had come to a personal accommodation with the king, which cost him a great deal of money. Wollaston, however, had gone from strength to strength since Violet had accused him of abusing his position. Wollaston served as "prime warden of his company, sheriff of London . . . [and] he was knighted in 1641."[12] Charles had knighted Wollaston after he had brought a petition to the king asking him to try to stay in London and help keep the peace. Charles hoped a knighthood would turn Wollaston into an ally, but Wollaston's sympathies lay with Parliament. He supported Parliament for religious reasons but also, no doubt, because Charles almost destroyed a major source of revenue for him when the king seized the Spanish silver in July 1640.[13]

In 1643, Wollaston was elected Lord Mayor of London. Unfortunately for Violet, his previous work undermining Wollaston made him a prime target when he neglected to pay his £70 tax bill. While not an enormous sum, it was still a substantial amount of money and placed Violet among the top 2 percent of rate payers. Wollaston decided to use Violet's delinquency to punish and humiliate him. On June 20, 1643, Parliament charged Violet with not paying his taxes and sent guards to arrest him and take him to Peter's House jail. Sometime later in the year, he was transferred to King's Bench jail. Violet's greed had now made him Parliament's prisoner.[14]

In prison Violet decided to join the Royalist cause. He realized that he and the king shared an enemy: the London goldsmiths. Violet hoped that, if he could help the king fight his war, Charles might very well reward him with the power to control the goldsmiths' trade. During his incarceration Violet made friends with two Royalist prisoners, named Sir Basil Brook and Colonel Read. Violet convinced Brook and Read that he knew all of the major players in London and that his opinion had weight in the merchant community. Brook and Read were impressed by Violet and introduced him to a secret Royalist agent—their jailer Theophilus Riley. After much discussion, the four men realized that if they worked together, they might succeed in devising a plot that could destroy Parliament and win the war for the king— which would of course bring great power and wealth to the four of them. [15]

Since theirs was a secret conspiracy the first thing they decided to do was invent code names that they used in all of their correspondence. Theophilus Riley, code-named "the Man in the Moon," would free Colonel Read, code-named "Lee," and Violet, code-named "James Morton." They exchanged letters, with salutation lines reading "Dear Man on the Moon," in which they developed their plot to use the London merchants to destroy Parliament's ability to wage war. Their scheme depended on severing Parliament's connection to its most important asset—money. While the high tax rates funded Parliament's war effort, the Roundheads often depended on loans from the merchants and goldsmiths of London to support them until the tax revenue came in. During the campaign season, the government used loans to pay for troops, weapons, and supplies. Without the merchants' and goldsmiths' help, Parliament would suffer a grievous blow—and maybe even a crippling one. [16]

The conspirators faced several dilemmas: how to get "James Morton" and "Lee" out of jail and, once they did that, how to connect the king, who was in Oxford, to the merchants in London. The courier would need special permission to travel between the two armies. Violet's jailer, Theophilus Riley, was a critical component of this part of the plan. His official title was "Scout Master of London," which gave him enough administrative clout to authorize a prisoner exchange that would free Violet and Read. Riley also could write a letter that would, for a legitimate reason, allow a Royalist delegation free passage into London. So Violet and Read—that is, "James Morton" and "Lee"—needed Riley, "The Man in the Moon," to release them from prison and write them a letter providing them safe passage.

Unfortunately for Violet, in November 1643, Theophilus Riley started to have second thoughts about the operation. Riley had not joined the conspiracy because he loved the king but for two other reasons—he wanted peace and he hated foreigners. His desire for peace was one that virtually everyone shared, but his hatred of foreigners can only be understood in the context of the military developments of 1643. In short, the war had generally gone very well for the Royalists in 1643, but Parliament's forces won enough victories by the end of the year that the Roundheads did not feel completely routed. [17] Yet, during most of the year, the parliamentary forces suffered setback after setback. The leader of the House of Commons, John Pym, had an idea of how Parliament's forces could receive help: unite with the Scots. In many ways this made sense. The Scots were fighting the king anyway, and they had an army full of battle-hardened veterans.

During the summer of 1643, Pym and Parliament negotiated with the Scots. The Scots were willing to help the English Parliament against the king, but they demanded a very high price. First, they required that the two kingdoms, Scotland and England, unite to form one administrative unit. This new nation would have the same religion: Presbyterianism. Religion weighed so heavily in the Scottish demands because the men who wrote the treaty between the two kingdoms were Scottish ministers. These men felt that it was God's will that everyone follow a Presbyterian church structure. For the English, this was problematic. By and large, in 1643, there were not many Presbyterians in England. Presbyterians were Calvinists who had an organization called the Kirk, which controlled their theology. The Kirk was made up of representatives of the various parishes, so it was not an Episcopal church structure where the clergy controlled everything from the top down. At this point, though, the English, who were Calvinists, tended to follow the congregational model as the Puritans did in New England, where each congregation determined its own theology.[18]

Thus when the Presbyterian Scots demanded that every adult Englishman swear an oath that would force them to embrace the Presbyterian model of religion, it was very difficult for the English to do so. Further, the oath, called the Solemn League and Covenant, had another aspect to it that made it hard to support.[19] The Scots demanded £30,000 a month to pay for their armies. Despite these stiff conditions, the English Parliament was desperate enough to pass the Solemn League and Covenant agreeing to Scottish demands on September 25, 1643.[20]

There were three reasons why this treaty would rub an Englishman like Theophilus Riley the wrong way. First, the cost was too high. The sum of £30,000 a month was a fortune, paid for by English taxes that had already skyrocketed during the war, and it did not seem fair to pay people who had invaded your country, regardless of which side they were on. Second, many Englishmen were not interested in a Presbyterian church structure. It became more popular in England as the 1640s wore on, but in 1643 this was not the case. Finally, the English were xenophobic. One of the most important pillars of their national identity was that they hated foreigners—all foreigners. Since the Scots were foreigners who had an army in England, if one supported the

Scots that meant supporting foreigners killing Englishmen in England, and that was simply too much to bear.[21]

Riley, then, was supporting the Royalists only because he hated the Scots more than he hated the Royalists. However, during November 1643 he could not decide if he wanted to help the Royalists. In an attempt to convince Riley to favor the king, Colonel Read wrote Riley letters (addressed to "the Man in the Moon") reminding Riley that the Scots were invading England and that the only way to bring peace to the country was to unite behind the king and defeat the foreign villains.[22] Read gave the letters to Violet, who delivered them to Riley in November 1643.

The evidence pushed Riley to help Violet in early December. Riley arranged a prisoner exchange with the Royalists. A Roundhead named Sir Arthur Haselrig, who was a very valuable Member of Parliament, was a POW in a Royalist fortress. Riley managed to exchange Read and Violet for Haselrig.[23] This brilliant move on Riley's part gave Violet a legitimate and legal reason to travel to Oxford, it provided Riley an excuse to grant Violet a pass that would go through the lines, and Parliament itself would have to approve it. When Riley filed the paperwork Violet was ready to travel from London to Oxford. On December 25, 1643, Violet got his pass from the House of Commons and went to his king.[24]

The conspiracy appeared to be on its way to success. Violet arrived the next day and met with George Digby, one of the king's closest advisors. Digby and the king supported the plan and they drafted a letter, to the merchants, that they wanted Violet to take back to London. Yet the conspirators neglected one important factor in their plans: Charles's weaknesses as a politician; his letter reveals many of them. First of all, he never apologizes to the merchants for the debacle of 1640, nor does he show that he understood why they might be mad at him. Instead, he writes that "notwithstanding the great defection we have found" in the city of London, he hoped that "all men are not so far degenerated from their affection to us . . . as to desire a continuance of the miseries they now feel." After insulting the merchants, he did not give them any compelling reason to join him. Rather, he said that for any "good subjects of that our city, whose hearts are touched with any sense of duty to us" that "we have thought fit to let you know; That we are ready to receive any such petition" that "may tend to the procuring a good understanding between us and that our City." In short, Charles told the merchants of London to make him an offer to help him, and if he thought that it was a good offer and that it did not insult his dignity, he might take it.[25] Charles did not know how to woo his subjects so he relied on threats and condescending rhetoric. His thought that this approach would work with the merchants of London illustrates why he drove his people to fight him in the first place.

On December 29, Charles gave Violet his poisoned letter and four days later, on January 2, 1644, Violet returned to London with it. He showed the letter to Sir David Watkins. Violet thought that Watkins was a closet Royalist, but in fact Watkins worked for Parliament. After discussing the letter with Watkins, Violet prepared to deliver the letter to the Common Hall in London, the meetingplace of many of the leading members of the London merchant community. At the Common Hall, Violet would present the king's message to some of the most important merchants in the city.[26] Yet all this time, Violet was being betrayed. Watkins told the goldsmiths that Violet was in town the very day he arrived, January 2, and the next day, the goldsmiths asked Violet to Goldsmiths' Hall to inform them about his recent meeting with the king. There, they interrogated him about what he had done, if he had traveled between the lines legally, and what role he played in the conspiracy to destroy the relationship between Parliament and the merchants in London. Starting to realize that he was being set up, Violet gave a vigorous defense. He argued that he had broken no laws whatsoever because there was no law that made it illegal to bring a peace proposal by the king to anyone. Violet also asserted that he had a legal warrant from Master Riley to move between the lines, and that if he would only testify on Violet's behalf, Riley would verify Violet's story. Finally, he noted that Master Riley had a great position of power in the City of London, granted to him by the Common Council of the City of London itself. And how could Violet not trust a man given such responsibility by the city's own government?[27]

Violet's fears intensified as he realized that the goldsmiths in the room regarded him as an enemy. Violet was right to be afraid because his enemies among the goldsmiths, particularly Sir John Wollaston, knew that Violet had now been upgraded in Parliament's eyes from a tax cheat to a traitorous spy intent on destroying representative government. Wollaston may have even been in the room, because Violet started making wild accusations, claiming that it was only because he had said the refiners for the mint (i.e., Wollaston) were illegally exporting gold and silver that the government was accusing him of wrongdoing.[28]

Yet Violet's own actions had damned him. By then, Parliament knew all of Violet's secret plans of the previous month and he and his fellow conspirators Sir Basil Brook, Colonel Read, and Theophilus Riley all faced treason charges. Within a week of meeting with the king in a daring move he thought might turn the English Civil War and elevate his own status, Parliament ordered that Violet be arrested and held a close prisoner in the Tower of London, the medieval fort in London that held the mint but also was a prison for the worst political enemies of the state. Often, prisoners like Violet would only be allowed to leave the Tower one way—by a public execution. Parliament did seriously consider executing Violet as a traitor and a spy. However, his crime was not deemed heinous enough for the death penalty. Instead Parliament did something almost worse than kill him—it took away his money.[29]

The sequestering of their estates was a common fate for Royalists in the English Civil Wars. It just hurt Violet more than most. His agent, Philip Cage, ran the manors he controlled, Battles Hall and Patton Hall; his mother and his sister held his cash and bonds. According to Violet, his total net worth at the time of his incarceration was £11,000. Over the next two years, Parliament took away the bonds and cash his mother had at her house and the bonds his sister had at her house, and it drove Cage off the manors. Parliament's agents also took the government positions he owned and sold them to someone else. The only time he was able to leave the Tower was to visit his seventy-seven-year-old mother as she was dying. Further, when he did get to visit Sara Vyolett, he was always under guard so could do nothing to tend to his affairs. (Only Thomas Violet would complain he could not make a business trip out of visiting his dying mother.) For Violet, the English Civil War had turned out to be very expensive indeed. Now faced with poverty, he spent most of his four years in the Tower thinking about what he loved the most but had no chance of acquiring—money.[30]

NOTES

1. The best recent summary of these events can be found in Austin Woolrych, *Britain in Revolution: 1625–1660* (Oxford: Oxford University Press, 2002) and Michael Braddick, *God's Fury, England's Fire* (London: Allen Lane, 2008).

2. Bucholz and Key, *Early Modern England 1485–1714*, 240–41.

3. Woolrych, *Britain in Revolution*, 64–65.

4. Bucholz and Key, *Early Modern England 1485–1714*, 241.

5. For an outstanding description and explanation of these events, see Braddick, *God's Fury, England's Fire*, chapters 1–9.

6. Keith Lindley, *Popular Politics and Religion in Civil War London* (Aldershot, UK: Scholar Press, 1997), 348–55.

7. *CSPD, 1640*, 465–66; *CSPD, 1640–41*, 524.

8. Woolrych, *Britain in Revolution*, 143.

9. *Journals of the House of Commons (CJ)*, vol. 2, 106.

10. Thomas Violet, *A True Discovery to the Commons of England* (London, 1650), 14–15.

11. Braddick, *God's Fury, England's Fire*, 269–70; Bucholz and Key, *Early Modern England, 1485–1714*, 254; S. R. Gardiner, *History of the Great Civil War 1642–1649*, vol. 1 (London: Longmans, Green, 1886), 269.

12. *Dictionary of National Biography (DNB)*, vol. 59, 988.

13. Challis, "Lord Hastings to the Great Silver Recoinage, 1464–1699," 275, 294; *DNB*, vol. 59, 988.

14. *CJ*, vol. 3, 136. For a fuller account of Violet's relations to Wollaston, see chapter 5. See Bucholz and Key, *Early Modern England 1485–1714*, 161, for Violet's income level.

15. Rushworth, *Historical Collections*, 379.

16. Ibid.

17. Woolrych, *Britain in Revolution*, 258–66.

18. Ibid., 270.

19. "The Solemn League and Covenant," in *The Constitutional Documents of the Puritan Revolution, 1625–1660*, 3rd ed., ed. S. R. Gardiner (Oxford: Oxford University Press, 1906), 267–71.

20. Bucholz and Key, *Early Modern England 1485–1714*, 255.

21. For an explanation of how Englishmen viewed foreigners, see Stoyle, *Soldiers & Strangers*. For another view of Riley's treason, see Lindley, *Popular Politics and Religion in Civil War London*, 247–48.

22. Violet, *The Advancement of Merchandize*, 136–38.

23. *DNB*, vol. 26, 874, does not indicate that Haselrig was ever a POW. However, the *Journals of the House of Commons (CJ)* indicate that Violet was traded for Haselrig. *CJ*, vol. 3, 353.

24. Violet, *The Advancement of Merchandize*, 138.

25. Thomas Violet, *To the Right Honourable the Lords in Parliament Assembled* (London, 1660), 3.

26. Rushworth, *Historical Collections*, vol. 5, 380–81.

27. Violet, *The Advancement of Merchandize*, 138–39.

28. Ibid., 139.

29. *CJ*, vol. 3, 359; Rushworth, *Historical Collections*, vol. 5, 381; Lindley, *Popular Politics and Religion in Civil War London*, 354; Gardiner, *History of the Great Civil War*, vol. 1, 269–70.

30. Violet, *The Advancement of Merchandize*, 142–43, 124–34; *CJ*, vol. 3, 686, 692. Violet never provides his sister's name.

Chapter Four

Economist

On January 6, 1644, Thomas Violet entered the Tower of London as a prisoner of the English Parliament. He would spend the next four years there. For most of that time, 928 days, in fact, he would be a "close prisoner in a dismal prison, little better than a dungeon."[1] Parliament did not release him from close confinement until about July 23, 1646, after which he had the freedom of the grounds and was not restricted to a small cell all day. However, he remained a prisoner in the Tower of London until October 1, 1647, when he was transferred to another jail. These were dark times for Violet. Prisoners in early modern England had to pay for their own accommodations. Wealthy inmates stayed in pleasant rooms with servants and could entertain visitors. Violet had money but he enjoyed no comforts. In fact, he spent £700 over nearly four years simply to keep himself alive. This was quite an outlay for staying in a dungeon. Meanwhile, the government was seizing his assets and selling them to help fund its war effort. Then, at the end of 1646, he fell ill and he thought he would die. He was so certain of this that he made a will that listed, among other things, all the people he thought owed him money.[2]

Throughout his time in the Tower of London, Violet stayed connected to his fellow prisoners and the king by sending and receiving letters through a sympathetic (or at least bribable) guard. They learned that the Royalist side lost the war in 1646 and that Charles and Parliament were negotiating a peace. During the peace talks in 1647, the treatment of Royalist prisoners in the Tower of London became a point of contention between the two sides. Because Violet and the other prisoners were communicating directly with Charles, it is very likely that an open letter that the prisoners published on

June 16, 1647, was part of a coordinated effort to raise their profile and to embarrass Parliament to cede this negotiating point to the king. To highlight the issue even further, on August 19, 1647, Charles sent two fat bucks to the prisoners in the Tower of London so they could hold a feast. One of the prisoners, Sir Francis Wortley, wrote a song for the occasion. Each stanza of the song described a different Royalist prisoner. While Wortley celebrated some of his fellow Royalists' courage, he said this about "Tom Violet."

> Tom Violet swears his injuries
> Are scarcely to be numbered;
> He was a close prisoner to the state
> These score days and nine hundred;
> For Tom does set down all the days,
> And hopes he has good debters;
> 'Twould be no treason (Jenkins says)
> To bring them peaceful letters.
> The king sent us. [3]

So while other Royalist POWs were bravely enduring their imprisonment, Tom Violet counted every day he was incarcerated and whined to everyone who spoke to him that he hoped the people who owed him money would pay him back. His stint in close confinement burned its way into his mind to the point that he painted the number "928" on the chimney in his room in the Tower of London to remind him how much time and money Parliament cost him. [4]

Once he had the freedom to move around the Tower of London during the day, Violet started looking for ways to improve his situation. His first move was to reach out to the king. Violet and Charles exchanged several letters about the political situation in the capital from 1645 to 1647. By September 1647, Parliament's forces held the king captive at his palace at Hampton Court, which is up the Thames River from London. Charles decided that he would rather escape and start another war than continue to negotiate with his enemies. Sometime during September 1647, the king came to believe that Thomas Violet might be able to help him in these designs. Charles ordered Violet to sneak himself out of the Tower of London, come to Hampton Court, and deliver some letters to him. One night that month Violet bribed a guard, "old White," to let him out on the premise that he was going drinking with friends. Violet made his way by boat up to Hampton Court where a couple of Charles's loyal servants hid him in the king's bedchamber behind some wall hangings. Over the next two hours, the king's guard came into the room several times and Violet trembled in fear. He was so scared and stiff when everyone left the room that he had trouble speaking when the king called him to come out. He managed to complete his mission, though, delivering letters that the king desperately wanted to read. Violet then carried letters detailing Charles's escape plan, which the king had written to another Royalist POW, named Lewis Dives. While Violet did not write the missives the king was reading, he had placed his life in jeopardy to bring them to the king in the hope that Charles would escape, fight again, win, and reward him.[5]

Violet risked his life to help the king because he thought it would help him in his dire financial situation. As his fellow Royalists had humorously noted, all Violet did was complain about his debt and how much money he was owed. In fact, except for writing a few letters about politics in London, during his years of close confinement he really had nothing else to do but think about money. Yet this bitter time actually provided Violet with an opportunity to do something he had never done before. He had time to think about not just making money for himself, but how everyone in England made money. In many ways, he stopped thinking like a merchant and a goldsmith and began thinking like an economist.[6]

During these years in the Tower of London, Violet began to develop his theory that free trade would lead to a more efficient, and hence more profitable, English economy. His ideas came from a combination of personal experience in trade during the 1630s, reflections on ongoing political and economic trends in England and Europe, and an understanding of what other economists had written about trade up to that point. And finally they emerged from his personal circumstances in the years 1644 through 1651. All of his insights appeared in 1651 when he published his seminal work on the subject, *The Advancement of Merchandize.*

Violet did not work in a vacuum. His ideas emerged not only from personal experience, but also from an unprecedented change in the way European economists viewed trade and the economy in general. Prior to the seventeenth century, when people discussed economics they were really talking about the weather. From the advent of agriculture through the sixteenth century, people assumed that the weather controlled the economy, and they were right. In self-sufficient agricultural societies, what mattered more than anything was the weather. If a farmer had enough rain and sun, in the right proportion, he enjoyed a good crop. The farmer then had enough to eat and he could save enough grain to plant during the next year. Yet if the weather was bad, he did not have enough to eat, and worse, not enough seed to plant during the next year. This led to hunger, starvation, sickness, and death.

In sixteenth-century Europe, this age-old pattern altered. For the first time since the fall of the Roman Empire, Europeans began trading large quantities of bulk commodities. People had been trading for centuries, but with a few exceptions, trade in the Middle Ages amounted to goods that only very rich people would buy—products like cinnamon, pepper, and silk. These luxury items would often travel thousands of miles—from China or the Spice Islands—all the way to Europe. However, since they were so small and expensive, they did not shape the lives of 99 percent of the population. But in the sixteenth century, new ships could sail in the Atlantic and connect northern European forests, North American fishing grounds, and South American silver to European consumers. Consequently, products like timber, grain, salt, wool, and silver were shipped in large quantities throughout Europe. By 1590, they were more important than the older trade in luxury goods.[7]

Europeans living in 1620 had experienced a full generation of this brave new world of commerce. The men who worked as the merchants realized that they lived in a different era than previous generations. Not only were thousands of people's livelihoods dependent on trade, but also the reasons why people prospered or suffered had less to do with self-sufficiency and more to do with a new phenomenon—the exchange of goods with strangers.

Take the example of fishermen. Dried fish (often cod) were some of the most valuable and important bulk commodities traded in Europe at this point. Fish could be easily dried and salted when caught and thus could be stored for months before people ate them. Further, people in Catholic countries in southern Europe could not eat meat on Fridays or during Lent so there was a great demand for fish in these countries. In the seventeenth century fishermen were catching most of their fish in northern European waters or off the coast of Newfoundland in North America. If in one year both North America and northern Europe yielded a bumper crop of fish, the southern European markets would be glutted with fish and the price would drop. While this was good for consumers in southern Europe, it was bad for fishermen. The fishermen, who had great success in catching huge amounts of fish, hardly would be paid anything. This did not make any sense. Why would a good year of fishing mean being paid less money? Further, since tens of thousands of men fished, it meant that hundreds of thousands of people were worse off because they caught too many fish.[8]

At first, Europeans were at a loss to explain why this happened. After all, they were used to thinking of their economic developments in terms of God's actions. If the weather was bad, the economy was bad. If the weather was good, the economy was good. Hence, if God was pleased with humans the weather would be good and people would have plenty to eat. This made sense. Now though, the weather could be good, fishermen could fill their nets, and then be worse off than in a year where the weather was bad and fish were scarce. The new reality was very hard to comprehend.

However, after dealing with this new world for a while, European thinkers began to put forward explanations for why things happened. They came to a rather frightening conclusion: The reason for economic developments— like gluts in the fish market—had nothing to do with God. Instead, it depended on the actions of men. Further, virtually all of the people involved in catching, processing, transporting, wholesaling, retailing, and consuming fish or any other bulk commodity did not live near each other. They spoke different languages, lived in different countries, and even followed different religions. It was very likely that a Scottish Presbyterian fisherman could sell his fish to a Dutch Jew who would be the middleman to vend the fish to Spanish Catholics. What English economists of the 1620s realized was that each group was dependent on others for the system to work.

Finally, because they were all living in different countries, an individual in the chain in fact had no control over the success of the transaction. A fisherman who caught a large bounty could lose money because of a glut in the market, or because of a war breaking out, or because a pirate raided a ship. This prospect was terrifying. To realize that the livelihood and wealth of tens of thousands of people depended on strangers' actions seemed to be the worst possible governing principle of trade.

Yet while people were scaring themselves to death over the realization of what large-scale bulk commodity trading was built upon, they also started developing a language for talking about it. Before this period, producers were more immediately connected and therefore, accountable, to consumers. For instance, if you grew wheat, you gave it to your miller, Frank Miller, to grind. You took the flour and made it into bread. If there was a problem with the supply chain, you need not imagine it—it was either your fault or Frank's. Now, though, a supply chain could involve a dozen parties, of whom you might know three. Men who wrote about economics understood this change, and it altered the way they talked about economic actions. Instead of describing economics as a personal action, writers now viewed it in the abstract. They started imagining the various links in supply chains and they started labeling them.[9] Thus, in the 1620s, the emergence of modern economic theory occurred when Europeans began to use abstract concepts and ideas to describe economic events.

Several writers, including the influential Thomas Mun, explained what these developments meant. A major shareholder in the East India Company, Mun wrote pamphlets, published in the 1620s and 1630s, that argued that trade should be allowed and encouraged to grow. That was the only way, said Mun, for the nation to get wealthier. Further, while individuals ran companies, trade was not run by anyone in particular—rather, as the economic historian Joyce Appleby wrote,

> [Mun] abstracted England's trade relations from their real context and built in that place an intellectual model. The shipment of goods, the exchange of bills, the trading of commodities became parts of an overall, unseen commercial flow, which moved independently of the specific, the person, and the concrete. For the first time economic factors were clearly differentiated from their social and political entanglements.[10]

Mun argued that Englishmen should embrace the new world of trade as the only possible way to enrich the nation—even if it meant submitting to the notion that they now operated in an economic environment that they only partially controlled.

These abstract concepts helped the English understand what was happening to their own economy in the 1620s. During that decade, three interrelated events converged to damage England's economy. First, a terrible war broke out in Europe—the Thirty Years' War (1618–48). The war most deeply affected central Europe, the final stop of England's most important export, wool. Thousands of English wool producers suffered terribly. Because European countries were desperate for money to pay for the war, they debased their currencies, which caused dreadful inflation. Finally, in the early part of the decade, bad weather meant that the harvests were poor and the price of food was very high. All three events combined to create a widespread discussion in the early 1620s over the issue of what was wrong with English trade.[11]

English thinkers were divided about what policy choices their government should make to navigate these treacherous waters. Some believed that the only way to thrive in the new economic world was to use free trade. Simply put, they felt that no one person or company should be allowed to control trade through taxes or monopolies. Free trade had had proponents for decades and by the 1620s it appealed to many writers as the cure to England's stagnant economy.[12] Others, though, argued that the government needed to help merchants control trade by establishing new structures to shape trade. The businesses they advocated for were usually joint stock companies, in which individual investors bought a share of the company, which spread the risk and the profit of an enterprise. They had developed in the sixteenth century, and by the early seventeenth century two joint stock companies in England were really taking off. The East India Company focused on trade with Asia; the Virginia Company, on the colonization of North America. While merchants had founded these companies and were their original investors, by the 1610s, English landowning aristocrats started becoming shareholders in these and similar corporations.

These corporations thrived for two reasons. First, the king gave them a monopoly on a certain part of the economy, which meant that they had no domestic competition. Second, by their very nature, joint stock companies spread risk. English investors came to believe that the way to deal with the new economic realities was to create joint stock companies that could take advantage of opportunities while reducing investors' exposure to losses. When joint stock companies were also monopolies, investors felt that they were dramatically increasing their chance to earn a profit.[13] These monopolies generated a fair amount of revenue for the king, and the shareholders also formed a potent lobby that argued for maintaining their special status. Meanwhile, other powerful men, like Secretary of State John Coke, argued that free trade would generate more revenue for the government. To experiment with a different strategy for increasing trade, the government made Dover a free port.[14]

It was in this economic and intellectual world that Violet became a player during the 1630s and 1640s. Violet understood that the new reality was frightening. Men and governments enjoyed making money from trade but feared the loss of control that they suffered because of it. Violet's writings always dealt with these paired issues: how to generate more revenue while at the same time increasing men's control of the new economy by regulating the nation's coin supply. His insight into these problems came from his experiences illegally exporting coins during the 1630s. Violet found that he could make money in two apparently contradictory ways—when he ignored the state's rules and when he enforced them. He formed these two opposing strategies while in prison and later developed them into a hypothesis on how the government could increase the flow of trade to England's benefit.

Violet argued that two things hindered trade: monopolies and taxes. The government made money in the 1630s by selling monopolies to joint stock companies. However, Violet realized that when one company controlled all English trade to a certain part of the world, it was bad for consumers. For instance, he noted that the Greenland Company (also called the Muscovy Company) monopolized trade with Greenland. Greenland did not have much to offer, but it did have one critical export commodity—oil made from whale blubber. The English used this oil for light. Since the Greenland Company had a monopoly on the importation of Greenland oil, it could charge whatever it wanted. If the government allowed competition, consumers would enjoy lower prices. This was also true of the Turkey Company, which controlled trade with the Ottoman Empire. The English purchased currants in large quantities from the Ottomans to use in cakes and puddings. The Turkey Company knew this and kept the price of currants high, which hurt the English consumer and the balance of trade (the ratio of English exports to imports). Violet, like everyone else in the seventeenth century, believed countries should export more than they imported and maintained that hurting the balance of trade weakened the overall economy.[15]

Violet did not like companies with monopolies because he thought that they were bad for consumers and the balance of trade. Further, he suffered from monopolies not only as a consumer, but also as a businessman. Violet learned this lesson personally when he was fighting with the gold refiners in the late 1630s. A group of eight refiners, under the leadership of John Wollaston, had a monopoly on refining all the precious metals that gold and silver wire drawers could purchase. Once Violet landed the post of overseer of the gold and silver wire drawers in 1638, he started a two-year battle with the refiners. He saw that the gold and silver wire drawers were much poorer (and hence he was much worse off) because they had to funnel all of their raw materials through only eight men's shops.[16]

Violet realized that his gold and silver wire drawers could improve their profits if they had more potential suppliers of gold. He also knew from his own trading earlier in the 1630s that open port cities made more money than port cities beset with many customs. He learned this at Dover when he was cheating Frenchmen out of their money. At the time, Dover was a free port; when foreign merchants arrived, they did not have to pay a special fee to dispense of their merchandise. Because of this policy, Dover became a clearinghouse. Foreign merchants docked in Dover, dropped off goods, stored them in warehouses, and shipped them back overseas to different markets when it was convenient. Violet found that in Dover there was ample work for poor people because they could help build warehouses and offload and load ships all the time. He concluded that "if you will let every man come in to Trade, according to their skill and abilities, that will, and let the rule be equal to all people in trade, let no man have a greater privilege than another," then everyone would be better off.[17] Meanwhile, so much material was going through the city every year that Violet claimed it earned "fifty thousand pounds" in customs revenue annually.[18]

This was Violet's state of mind when, on October 1, 1647, he was released from the Tower of London and sent to King's Bench jail. He never says exactly when the government finally released him from King's Bench, but he did complain that he was incarcerated, all told, more than seven years. If true, he was released sometime in the middle of 1649. Certainly by July 1649 he was in Essex, trying to get his property back.[19] Whatever his exact release date, Violet came out into a world very different from the one he had left in January 1644. During the five years he was in custody, Parliament had won the Civil War and used its high taxes to pay for a new type of army—the New Model Army, a force where men were promoted by merit (instead of birth) and trained before they entered combat. Parliament had put together a military force that was better paid, disciplined, and led than the Royalist armies. By 1646, Parliament had won the war and the king had fled to the Scottish army because he thought that he would receive better peace terms from the Scots than the English. The Scots, though, needed money to pay for their army and found it when their leaders sold Charles to the English Parliament for £400,000.[20]

Now in the custody of the Parliament of England, Charles began negotiating a peace settlement in 1646 and 1647. There were many unresolved questions between the two sides: How much authority should Parliament have? What role would the king play in the government? Would they all become Presbyterians as they had promised the Scots earlier in the war? Parliament and the king spent 1646 and 1647 arguing about these issues. Charles, though, never negotiated in good faith. He wanted to be the supreme ruler of England and refused to give in to any of Parliament's demands. He tried to escape from Parliament's custody repeatedly, failing in every attempt. Finally Charles decided that he should start another war. Even though he was still Parliament's prisoner, in 1648 he gave secret approval to the Royalists in

England to begin an uprising against the Parliament. Ironically, during the 1648 war the Royalists allied with the Scots who thought that Parliament was not going to follow through with its promises about religious reform. This second civil war explains why the English speak of the "English Civil Wars" rather than the "English Civil War." Parliament's forces won this second war, too, as its army—the New Model Army—crushed the Royalists and the Scots.

Members of Parliament and especially officers in the army were so angry at Charles, who was under their control this whole time, for starting the second civil war that they started contemplating an entirely new course of action. Previously they thought that they could keep Charles as king, with his power curtailed. Now, some members of Parliament and the army decided that Charles should not rule at all, but rather be executed. The members of Parliament who did not agree with this extreme course were purged on December 6, 1648, by Colonel Thomas Pride's troops—an event that went down in English history as Pride's Purge. Over the next two months, the Purged Parliament set up a special tribunal to try Charles for treason against his own people. The court found him guilty, and on January 30, 1649, Charles Stuart was brought out of the Banqueting House onto a scaffold, where an executioner cut off his head in front of a large crowd.

Two months later, Parliament proclaimed England a Commonwealth, the only time in their history that the English experimented with republicanism. The Commonwealth faced many enemies. English Royalists, willing to ally with anyone now, came together with Irish Catholics and Scottish Presbyterians (who believed Parliament should not have executed the king) to fight against the new government. From 1649 to 1651 the new regime fought these combined forces. Oliver Cromwell, Parliament's major general, led English armies into Ireland and Scotland. In 1649, Cromwell's forces crushed and massacred the Irish in a campaign that still resonates in Ireland today. Then, in Scotland in 1650, Cromwell's army showed that the famous Scottish troops were no match for the New Model Army at the Battle of Dunbar. Finally, in the late summer of 1651, the Royalists in Scotland tried one last desperate attempt to invade England, but Cromwell's forces caught them in Worcester on September 3, 1651, and destroyed them. The English Parliament had now conquered not only England, but Scotland and Ireland as well.[21]

During these years of intense political and military drama, there were also major economic developments that would shape the history of the 1650s, the

English Commonwealth, and Thomas Violet's career as an economic thinker. The key event that determined all others was the end of the Thirty Years' War in 1648. The war had hurt and then helped the English economy. In the 1620s, disruptions of trade slowed English exports, but then in the 1630s and 1640s, they created new opportunities for two reasons. The Dutch, the most advanced traders in Europe at this time, fought against the Spanish during these decades. The war severely crippled Dutch shipping and the English managed to take their place as the linchpin in European trade. Then there was the Spanish silver. As noted in chapter 3, since the Dutch and the Spanish were fighting each other, they could not trade directly. Spanish merchants, who had huge amounts of silver from their South American colonies but did not manufacture many goods, desperately needed Dutch manufactured goods. To purchase them during the war, these merchants sent their silver to England, where the English mint minted the silver into English coins. English merchants shipped the coins to the Netherlands where they purchased Spanish goods, then sent the goods back to England for the Spanish to pick them up. (It was this silver that Charles tried to take in July 1640.) This roundabout trade was incredibly profitable for the English.

When the Thirty Years' War ended, it was fantastic news for the wider European economy because trade could flow across the continent once more. It hurt the English, though, because it allowed the Dutch to trade with everyone again. The Dutch were enjoying what their historians call "the Golden Age," having discovered many of the principles of capitalism before everyone else—including the English. The Dutch had free cities, where merchants from all over Europe could trade without paying customs taxes. The Dutch had also perfected joint stock companies. When Dutch investors bought into a joint stock company, they could sell their shares of the company only when they found a buyer. In short, their investment would remain part of the company's capital. In England, investors received all of their returns once the particular voyage that they had invested in was completed. The Dutch, with far more available capital, could build many more ships than their English competitors. Thus, the Dutch made more ships, had more money, and manufactured more goods than the English. In 1648, they could now freely trade with all of Europe, which was a disaster for the English because "no sooner did Spain and the Dutch make peace than the bubble of England's prosperity burst."[22] The Dutch took over almost all of the Mediterranean and Baltic trade from the English. To add insult to injury, "the transmission of Spanish silver for Flanders through England simply stopped dead as the Madrid bankers switched over to Amsterdam." Dover ceased to be an important port, and English trade all but collapsed. [23]

English merchants and government now faced a twofold crisis. First, everyone working in international trade was seriously hurt and unemployment and bankruptcies exploded in this sector of the economy. Then, at the same time, the English were quite literally starting to run out of money. Without a steady supply of Spanish silver, the English mint did not have any bullion to mint into coins. Without new coins, people would only pass old, worn, and clipped money. It meant less trust in the money in circulation, hurting commerce.

Violet did not react to these economic developments in 1648 and 1649. During those years, he was desperately trying to recover the land and money that Parliament had taken from him in the early years of his imprisonment. He made his case to every court and every jurisdiction that would listen, from London to Essex. In each circumstance, though, he was turned down. As a Royalist spy, he would never be given back any of his money or his land. With no revenue and no prospects for employment, Violet had to live off of loans. Angry, poor, and desperate, Violet watched the major political events of 1649 pass him by as his once bright prospects faded away.

In the middle of the spring of 1650, Violet realized a new way forward. He had to become a supporter of the English Republic. At this point, Royalist forces still controlled Scotland and it was not clear if they could be defeated. While a risky move on Violet's part, he knew that the only way he could earn a living was to change his political tune and support the new government. On May 22, 1650, Parliament debated the lack of coins and the collapse of trade. Violet followed the discussion closely and saw he had the perfect opportunity to prove to the members of Parliament that he was now on their side. He could show them how the economy worked, and what to do to improve it, and, finally, he could explain how currency functioned. He had thought about the former while in prison and he had thought about the latter all his life. He could show Parliament how to save itself and the nation, and then he would begin earning money again. [24]

On May 29, 1650, Violet presented a very long petition to the Council of State, the executive body in the Republic. The House of Commons debated all bills and had to act to pass laws, but the Council of State actually ran the day-to-day activities of the government. Violet knew that if he could convince its members that he could help them, he would get the black mark off his name and start earning money again. Violet opened with a slogan: "Commerce is the life of a State, manufactures are the sinews of trade, and money is the soul of both."[25] By linking the power of the state and private business, Violet hoped to attract the attention of various constituencies in the council. Further, by echoing Mun, the famous economist, Violet revealed he understood the basic principles underlining current economic theory. It would also, he hoped, allow him to provide judicious criticism of the government's political policies. Violet explained that "the first and principal reason of the decay of trade has been the late unhappy wars."[26] Violet also acknowledged the continuing wars in Ireland and Scotland cost "a very considerable sum." The problem with this policy of military engagement and occupation in foreign parts was that the tax money that the English raised was spent in Ireland and Scotland rather than in England. Armies at the time paid for their supplies in the field instead of bringing food with them. Since the most important expenditure of an army was purchasing food, the English government was spending its money helping Scottish and Irish farmers.[27]

While the wars were bad for the economy, there was also an enemy within. Violet wrote that "retailers and shopkeepers take liberties to become merchants, as many have done of late years, under pretense of liberty and free trade."[28] According to Violet, shopkeepers did not have the ability to trade with foreigners. (Violet viewed shopkeepers as retailers, merchants as wholesalers. Shopkeepers did not understand international trade.) Shopkeepers overpaid for foreign goods and then grossly undersold English goods abroad. Their incompetence sent English coin abroad just when the country was in dire need of currency.[29] The Dutch exacerbated the English currency shortage because they could now directly sell their goods to the Spanish, "silver and pieces of 8" (a Spanish gold coin) now "go to Holland" rather than England.[30] Without a decent supply of silver for the mint the English economy was sputtering due to the lack of available currency and might soon stop. Violet's description of the problems facing the English economy matches historians' views today. In short, to the best of our knowledge, Thomas Violet thoroughly understood the economic problems facing England in 1650. Further, his presentation before the Council of State clearly convinced the members of the council that he knew what he was talking about because they could not wait to hear his solutions to their pressing dilemmas.

Violet proposed a series of political and economic ideas that he thought would not only aid the English economy, but also help the English Republic earn some political capital with its citizens. Violet suggested that the republic end "free quarter," the practice of housing soldiers in people's homes with the expectation that they be given lodging and food. It amounted to an extra tax on the English people, because they were virtually never refunded for their expense. Then, Violet suggested that Parliament pass an Act of Oblivion, which would erase all sins people committed during the late wars and allow everyone to start over. This would help Violet, of course, but it would also encourage the country go about the business of reconciliation and peace rather than continue with old squabbles.[31]

After addressing these political issues, Violet told the Council of State how to improve the economy. He thought that "For [the] recovery of trade and commerce, the merchants need encouragement and protection from the State." Merchants, not shopkeepers, should be unregulated and be allowed to freely trade with the whole world. Violet noted this was exactly what the Dutch government was doing, and it had allowed the Dutch merchant community to build up an enormous merchant marine that dominated the fishing industries and international trade. Violet wrote that in the Netherlands itself, "they have not wood of their own to warm themselves in winter." Yet because "they abound in quality and quantity of all manufactures . . . they fetch the materials thereof from all other parts of the world, which are so much improved by their policy and industry, that they eat out other nations that trade with them."[32]

Violet then addressed the problem of the money supply. He noted that Sir John Wollaston, "Mr. Alderman," had told Parliament how to manage the gold supply in the country but also said that "it is a mystery beyond his understanding."[33] Violet said that the government needed someone in charge of the money supply who could not only understand it, but also explain it and then solve the problem of the disappearance of precious metals in England. Violet suggested that Parliament follow his protocol. He argued that it should pass an act that would allow importers to bring gold and silver into Dover and not pay tax on two thirds of it. He then recommended that the gold and silver should be quickly minted into coins, but the merchants who brought the gold and silver should be given a very good deal—charging them only "2s. [shillings] the lb. troy of silver and 15s. gold."[34] Finally, Violet maintained that the English needed to make exports as cheap as possible because then foreigners' money would flow into England. At the moment, the Dutch were using this strategy and capturing all of England's foreign trade. If the English government followed his advice, Violet assured the Council of State that it would ensure a steady supply of gold and silver coins for the mint, facilitating domestic trade and dramatically increasing international trade for English merchants.[35]

Almost as soon as Violet was finished presenting his plan, the Council of State responded. The members immediately said that "the Commissioners of Customs" had to prevent the export of bullion from England. In order to make this happen, "it may be beneficial to allow Mr. Violet a halfpenny in the pound for what bullion he shall discover in any merchant's hands, not intended for the Mint." This statement did not mean Violet had landed a position overseeing gold and silver exports, but the committee did recommend him for it.[36]

Events moved quickly. Violet presented himself to the Council of State on May 29, heard the members' response on May 30, and almost certainly the next day they asked him to spy for them. The council was divided between those who liked his plan and those who did not. One person who supported his idea was John Bradshaw, the president of the Council of State. He had been the lead judge at the trial of Charles I and was one of the most important men in the new government. Bradshaw told Violet that if he could convince the council how his plans would improve the health of the Commonwealth, Violet might be able to get his estate back.[37] Inspired, Violet spent the month of June writing a pamphlet that outlined his economic ideas that he hoped would both explain to the Council of State why those ideas would lead to economic growth and, ultimately, help him regain his estates. On July 15, 1650, he published his pamphlet titled *A True Discovery to the Commons of England.* The subtitle was "How they have been cheated of almost all the Gold and Silver coyn of this nation" and "How the people of this Nation, are, and have been abused by light and clipped English money, and the means shewed for the prevention thereof." *A True Discovery to the Commons of England* revealed that Violet understood the inner workings of the mint, the role of the goldsmiths in England's money supply, and how he combined his theoretical and practical knowledge with his relentless need for self-promotion.

In this pamphlet Violet also aligned himself with one of the factions in Parliament: the Independents. During the Civil War, the Roundheads in Parliament broke into two groups called Presbyterians and Independents. The Presbyterians were the larger group and generally wanted a Presbyterian Church structure. They were also willing to try to come to an accommodation with the king. Independents wanted independent churches (meaning no government oversight over individual congregations) and opposed an agreement with the king. While the Presbyterians were the majority in the House of Commons, the Independents were the majority in the army—particularly among the officers. During Pride's Purge in December 1648, the Independents in the army and Parliament colluded to remove the Presbyterians from Parliament. Thus, the men who killed Charles and established the Republic were almost all Independents who felt that the English Presbyterians did not have the nerve to really run the government.

Since Bradshaw was an Independent, Violet decided he would show Bradshaw he was, too. In his pamphlet, Violet unveiled a new reason why he was incarcerated in January 1644. He announced that a Presbyterian plot had ruined him. Violet claimed that the Presbyterians in Parliament knew that coal from Newcastle (a northern town that was then the major source of London's coal, used for cooking and heating) sold in London for nine or ten shillings a ton. Once the Presbyterians' Scottish allies took Newcastle, though, the English Presbyterians arranged for London's coal to come from Scotland, which cost thirty or forty shillings per ton—or a 400 percent increase. Violet then claimed that because he petitioned Parliament about this crime, the Presbyterians in Parliament arrested him and imprisoned him for nearly four years. Of course, one of the most important Presbyterians in London in 1643 was Sir John Wollaston, the Lord Mayor.[38] There is no evidence to corroborate this story at all. Certainly there were wartime shortages in 1643–44, but the Presbyterians in London were not mad at Violet because he was talking about coal prices. Rather, the goldsmiths and gold and silver wire drawers were angry with him because he kept informing on them to the king. The tale Violet wove for Bradshaw was designed to prove that Violet supported him rather than Presbyterians like Wollaston.

Violet's pamphlet did not shape the debate on trade primarily because it only focused on gold production. Bradshaw, though, who spoke to Violet, wanted Violet to air not just his views about gold production, but also his economic theory on free trade. Bradshaw asked Violet to write another pamphlet. This time, Bradshaw helped promote it by allowing Violet to use William Dugard's printing press. Dugard was the printer to the Council of State and anything he printed would have the clear backing of powerful men in the government. This pamphlet, called *The Advancement of Merchandize: or Certain Propositions for the Improvement of the Trade of this Commonwealth to the Right Honorable the Council of State*, appeared on February 17, 1651.[39]

It is here that Violet most clearly and explicitly makes his argument about how trade should work. Because England "hangs in the Sea, like an Oriental Pearl at a fair Ladie's ear," ships could come to England from any direction and go forth anywhere in the world. Such a natural advantage meant that "free trade will treble the Importation and Exportation of goods into all the sea ports of this nation" and dramatically increase employment in port cities.[40]

Violet then goes on to explain how this would work. It was similar to his thoughts in the Tower of London but updated to deal with current economic and political developments. The government should allow two things—free trade and the right for foreigners to trade freely in England. These steps would lead to a dramatic expansion of trade by allowing both English and foreign merchants to come to England and exchange their goods in the free-trade ports. Violet envisioned thousands of Englishmen finding work off-loading and loading ships and working in warehouses, as well as outfitting and repairing the ships that came into the ports. Foreign merchants would come to the ports because they did not have to pay special taxes and they would like to be in England since it was well situated to send goods anywhere in Europe on short notice. Violet reminded the English authorities that the Dutch, who were poor in natural resources, managed to defeat the Spanish after an eighty-year war, build a massive trade empire in the East and West Indies, and have the most important market in Europe at Amsterdam because they had free trade that allowed foreign merchants easy access to their cities. The English should copy this successful model and return to prosperity.[41]

Violet had two other insights he shared with his readers. Tariffs and taxes reduced wealth. He noted that Spain, which had all the wealth of its New World silver mines at its disposal, was always short of money. Violet explained this happened because the Spanish had raised the "Custom of Silver" from "two . . . to five, six, eight, ten, twelve, fifteen *per cent*." The dramatic increase in customs on their silver imports actually decreased the Spanish government's revenue because Spanish merchants who brought the silver in from the New World anchored their ships beyond Spain's jurisdiction at "the Bay of Saint Lucar" and there they took "out their Silver and rich Commodities, and ship[ped] it for other parts of the world, before it paid one pennie Custom, or touched the Spanish shore." The foolish Spanish then, who had more silver than any other country on earth, found themselves without silver coins to spend in their own country. Violet likened their predicament to the "proverb . . . which saith, who goe's worse shod than the shoo-maker's wife."[42]

If high taxes led to less trade, so did xenophobia. Violet constantly emphasized the importance of foreign merchants to English trade. Violet knew that many foreign merchants, called "Merchant Strangers," were critical components to his plan to increase English trade. Violet went further, and claimed that if all "these Merchant Strangers, such as abide here [in England] with their Families, were Naturalized" the entire nation would benefit. England would gain valuable citizens if "the Dutch" Merchant Strangers could "all [be] turned into English." The son of a Dutch immigrant himself, Violet listed thirty-five Dutch men who he felt should be immediately given English citizenship. He argued that by naturalizing the Dutch into Englishmen, they would "bestow . . . on the English Nation" all of the "Wealth they have gotten" in their various enterprises.[43]

Violet's ideas resonated. He was not the only writer advocating for free trade—in fact men had been doing so for decades.[44] By 1651, though, many merchants agreed that the monopolies of the various companies hurt consumers and the overall economy. Further, it was very clear that by opening up English ports to non-company shipping—in effect embracing the free trade Violet advocated—trade would increase and prosperity would come again to the English. Inspired by these ideas, during the spring of 1652, traders and fishermen tried to break the Muscovy Company's and the Turkey Company's monopolies on trade.[45] That same year, the Council of State approved a pamphlet, written by Benjamin Worsley, that celebrated the opportunities of free trade. Worsley cited Violet in his pamphlet—twice.[46]

Yet perhaps the most important contribution Violet made came unexpectedly, with the passage of the Navigation Act of 1651. Historians consider the Navigation Act to be one of the most important pieces of economic legislation passed by the English Parliament in the whole early modern period. Throughout the first half of the seventeenth century, English merchants, policy makers, and economists were divided over the role that the state should play in promoting trade. Generally speaking, as we saw earlier in this chapter, the state had supported individual companies' monopolies over a certain product or region (as with the East India Company). In October 1651, however, Parliament chose to go in another direction. It decided that England should follow the Dutch model. Parliament "create[d] an overarching national monopoly within which English shipping and long-distance trade could develop—especially the re-export trades in colonial and Asian staples." The

Navigation Act was the beginning of a long struggle between individual monopolies and the larger merchant community to determine how the English would orient their economy. After 1689 the proponents of the Navigation Act won (with a few exceptions) and their ideas guided English and British policymaking through the end of the eighteenth century.[47] Their plan was almost exactly what Violet argued for in February 1651.

Violet, however, is virtually never mentioned in the context of the Navigation Act. Instead, an August 1651 pamphlet by Benjamin Worsley titled *The Advocate* has been cited numerous times as the justification for the Navigation Act.[48] The reason historians cite Worsley's pamphlet and not Violet's is that *The Advocate* is an anti-Dutch tirade. It warns that the Dutch are dominating English shipping and trade, and that the English must act to keep the Dutch out.[49] Instead of emulating the Dutch, as Violet argued in February 1651, the English had to defend themselves against them because they were an almost existential threat to the English economy. Since the First Anglo-Dutch War (1652–54) broke out only a few months after the Navigation Act passed, it is little wonder that the overwhelming scholarly consensus about the Navigation Act was that it was passed to spite the Dutch. While there is some dispute whether it passed because of political, economic, or religious reasons, there is no argument about Violet's contribution to the act. He is simply ignored.[50]

No doubt Violet is not considered an important contributor to the Navigation Act because he promoted a pro-Dutch, rather than an anti-Dutch, position. Violet went even further, however, than simply supporting "the Dutch" generally. He highlighted the achievements of individual Dutchmen and their potential contributions to the English Commonwealth. Most notably, he asked that "James Stenirs," a Dutch merchant living in England, be allowed to be naturalized as an English citizen. Violet believed that Stenirs, as Violet spelled his name, would help the English prosper if he was allowed to join their Commonwealth. Imagine Violet's chagrin when in December 1652 James Steneer, also known as Jacomo Staneir (the Dutch spelling of his name; notice Violet's spelling is more Dutch than English) was captured as a Dutch spy living in London during the Anglo-Dutch War. Steneer planned to corrupt the highest levels of English government in order to help the Dutch win the war (see chapter 6).[51] Since Violet had supported a dangerous spy—in print, no less—everything he advocated for was suspect.

Yet while Violet's Dutch connections certainly were out of step with the mainstream opinion in 1651–52, Worsley still cited Violet's *The Advance-*

ment of Merchandize in his 1652 pamphlet titled *Free Ports, the Nature and Necessitie of them Stated.* Worsley, who worked for the Council of Trade, which consulted with and took direction from the Council of State, may have been ordered to write his 1652 pamphlet in order to explain the benefits of the Navigation Act. For while Parliament passed the act because leading members were angry at the Dutch, its passage "represented a genuine departure in public policy." By setting up a system where the national government helped facilitate trade for the whole country, rather than simply individual companies, it transformed the English commercial landscape.[52]

Violet was not credited with any of the ideas that led to this achievement. Supporters of the Navigation Act wanted to avoid Violet at all costs as his own reputation kept them from acknowledging his contributions to their cause. In fact, while Benjamin Worsley used Violet's writings in his pamphlet supporting free trade, he never once mentioned Violet's name. Worsley avoided crediting Violet not just because of the Dutch connection, but also because so many people hated him. The Presbyterians involved in government detested his attacks on them and opposed his ideas for partisan reasons. Then there were those who rejected his ideas simply because of who he was. For Violet had not changed. His goal was still to make money off of other people's mistakes. Too many people knew that Violet "was a sly and dangerous fellow" who "is always presenting Propositions unto us which may bear double interpretations."[53] Violet may have convinced Bradshaw that free trade was a sure path to prosperity, but too many people thought it would just give the pro-Dutch, former Royalist, anti-Presbyterian Thomas Violet another means of manipulating others for his benefit and their loss. Since all of his previous ideas were plays for his own gain, it is not surprising that critics would feel this way. Violet's own behavior ensured he would be actively forgotten by contemporary writers and historians alike.[54]

NOTES

1. Violet, *To the Right Honourable the Lords in Parliament Assembled*, 1.

2. Violet, *The Advancement of Merchandize*, 142–43; Violet, *To the Right Honourable the Lords in Parliament Assembled*, 1; PROB 20/2650.

3. Francis Wortley, "A Loyall Song" ([16 Sept.] 1647), in *Political Ballads Published in England during the Commonwealth*, vol. 3, ed. Thomas Wright (London: Percey Society, 1841), 97. See also 87–88 for background information. The Jenkins mentioned in the song was Judge Jenkins, a Royalist judge who gave legal advice to incarcerated Royalists.

4. Violet, *A Petition against the Jews* (London, 1660), second part, 31.

5. Violet, *A Petition against the Jews*, 28–32; for the king's time in Hampton Court and plotting, see S. R. Gardiner, *History of the Great Civil War*, vol. 3 (London: Longmans, Green, 1889), 354; Gardiner, *History of the Great Civil War*, vol. 4 (London: Longmans, Green, 1894), 2. These events had to have occurred in September because Charles only came to Hampton Court on August 24 and Violet was transferred out of the Tower of London on October 1, 1647. See Gardiner, vol. 3, in this note and *CJ*, vol. 5, 322. Of course, since the only source of these events is Violet himself, we might question the details—or even the entire story of bringing the letters to Charles.

6. Violet, *The Advancement of Merchandize*, Sig. b, for evidence he developed his economic ideas in the Tower of London.

7. Jonathan Israel, *Dutch Primacy in World Trade, 1585–1740* (Cambridge: Cambridge University Press, 1989), 6–8. For a different view of late medieval commerce, see Peter Spufford, *Power and Profit: The Merchant in Medieval Europe* (New York: Thames and Hudson, 2002), 228–341.

8. See Israel, *Dutch Primacy in World Trade*, 24, for an example of how fishing expanded in the sixteenth century.

9. Joyce Oldham Appleby, *Economic Thought and Ideology in Seventeenth-Century England* (Princeton, NJ: Princeton University Press, 1978), 20. The summary of economic theory comes from Appleby's excellent book, chapters 2 and 3.

10. Ibid., 41.

11. Ibid., 35–36; John Pym, "A Commons Debate of the Trade Depression, Recorded by John Pym, 26 February, 1621," cited in *Seventeenth-Century Economic Documents*, eds. Joan Thirsk and J. P. Cooper (Oxford: Oxford University Press, 1972), 1–2.

12. Men had been arguing in support of free trade since the sixteenth century. See Yerby, *The English Revolution and the Roots of Environmental Change*, 148–53. For the early seventeenth century, see *CSPD, 1603–1610*, 315; *CSPD, 1619–1623*, 477.

13. Bucholz and Key, *Early Modern England*, 202–3.

14. *CSPD, 1640–41*, 367; for Coke's being convinced of the merits of free trade, see Prideaux, *Memorials of the Goldsmiths' Company*, 175–78.

15. Violet, *The Advancement of Merchandize*, 9–10.

16. Ibid., 106–10.

17. Ibid., 11.

18. Ibid., 2–3.

19. Violet, *Petition against the Jews*, 18; British Library Additional Manuscript, 33925, 40r.

20. Braddick, *God's Fury, England's Fire*, 473.

21. For an excellent summary of these events, see Woolrych, *Britain in Revolution*, chapters 11, 12, 13, 14, 15.

22. Israel, *Dutch Primacy in World Trade*, 199.

23. Ibid., 200.

24. *CSPD, 1650*, 178.

25. Ibid., 179.

26. Ibid., 178.

27. Ibid., 179.

28. Ibid.

29. Ibid., 179–80.

30. Ibid., 182.

31. Ibid., 180.

32. Ibid.

33. Ibid.

34. Ibid., 181.

35. Ibid., 181–82.

36. Ibid., 182.

37. Violet, *The Advancement of Merchandize*, Sig. A2r.

38. Violet, *A True Discovery to the Commons of England*, 17–18.

39. Violet, *The Advancement of Merchandize*, title page.

40. Ibid., Sig. a2r.

41. Ibid., 1–6, 23–24.

42. Ibid., 4–5.

43. Ibid., 17.

44. Yerby, *The English Revolution and the Roots of Environmental Change*, 148–61.

45. *CSPD, 1651–52*, 177, 178, 232, 235, 271.

46. Benjamin Worsley, *Free Ports, the Nature and Necessitie of them Stated* (London, 1652), 4, 8.

47. David Ormond, *The Rise of Commercial Empires: England and the Netherlands in the Age of Mercantilism, 1650–1770* (Cambridge: Cambridge University Press, 2003), 31–32, quote on 32. See also Robert Brenner, *Merchants and Revolution: Commercial Change, Political Conflict, and London's Overseas Traders, 1550–1653* (Cambridge: Cambridge University Press, 1993), 625–28. For the text of the Navigation Act, see S. R. Gardiner, ed., *The Constitutional Documents of the Puritan Revolution* (Oxford: Oxford University Press, 1906), 468–71.

48. J. E. Farnell, "The Navigation Act of 1651, the First Dutch War, and the London Merchant Community," *Economic History Review* 16, no. 3 (1964): 439–54, esp. 439–40; Steven Pincus, *Protestantism and Patriotism: Ideologies and the Making of English Foreign Policy, 1650–1688* (Cambridge: Cambridge University Press, 1996), 48.

49. Benjamin Worsley, *The Advocate* (London, August 1652), 1–14. See Thomas Leng, *Benjamin Worsley (1618–1677): Trade, Interest, and the Spirit in Revolutionary England* (Woodbridge, UK: Royal Historical Society, 2008) for a fascinating recent biography of Worsley.

50. For an excellent summary of the historiography of the Navigation Act, see Pincus, *Protestantism and Patriotism*, 11–14, 40–50.

51. Violet, *The Advancement of Merchandize*, 17; *CJ*, vol. 7, 223–24.

52. Appleby, *Economic Thought and Ideology*, 103.

53. Violet, *An Appeal to Caesar*, 54.

54. Worsley, *Free Ports*, 4, 8. Violet was not completely forgotten by historians. In 1972 Joan Thirsk and J. P. Cooper included several of Violet's writings in their book, *Seventeenth-Century Economic Documents*, 57–63, 519–20, 724–25.

Chapter Five

Trappaner

Late in his life, one of Violet's enemies called him a "trappaner." According to the *Oxford English Dictionary*, the archaic word meant "an entrapper, decoy, swindler."[1] One of Violet's goals in the early 1650s was to entrap and swindle Sir John Wollaston. Violet's motives were not simply financial; he wanted revenge against Wollaston for his role in Violet's incarceration in the winter of 1643–44. Violet hoped to achieve both aims by taking ownership of two plum positions Wollaston held—he was the melter for the mint and the holder of the monopoly as the supplier of gold and silver to the gold and silver wire drawers. To do this, Violet had to set a trap for Wollaston, destroy him politically, and prove he was a criminal.

Achieving his grand ambition required hard work and luck because Wollaston was a powerful man. Wollaston started off in a higher position in life than Violet. Born around 1585 at Tettenhall, Staffordshire, he was the second son of a gentleman. His parents, Edward and Elizabeth Wollaston, believed that the best way their younger son could thrive in the world was to go into trade. They decided to make him a goldsmith. It was a wise choice; banking and the production of money was one of the most secure means of earning a generous income. In 1604, Wollaston started his apprenticeship for the London goldsmith Edward Green. These must have been happy years for him. He met his future wife at Green's home, Green's daughter Rebecca. In 1611, Wollaston became a freeman of the Goldsmiths' Company, and married Rebecca in 1616. Wollaston was a hard worker and he knew how to make the best of social networking. In 1622, he was already an important man in the Goldsmiths' Company and well liked by most of his peers. By the mid-

1620s, Wollaston had been his own master for a decade and a half and knew the ins and outs of his trade. Due to his skills and connections he was a natural fit for one of the most lucrative positions a goldsmith could hold in London, which was melter for the Royal Mint, a position he received in 1624.[2]

The melter of the Royal Mint was the subcontractor responsible for melting all the gold and silver before it was cast into coins. The melter's superior was the Master of the Mint, a political appointee who usually did not really understand the mint. Therefore, the Master left the real work to Wollaston. Wollaston oversaw the manufacturing of millions of pounds of coins in the three decades he served as melter. His contract stated that he would be paid six pence per pound of gold melted and two pence per pound of silver melted. Every year, Wollaston's workers processed a fortune in silver and gold. For instance, in the year from April 1, 1631, to March 31, 1632 (the Royal Mint's fiscal year), Wollaston's men transformed 3,544 pounds of gold into coins with a face value of £145,310. They also processed 21,788 pounds of silver into £67,545 worth of coins. As the amount of Spanish silver increased over the 1630s, the amount of silver the mint processed grew. In fiscal year 1637–38, for instance, Wollaston melted 169,387 pounds of silver, which netted £525,101.[3] At a payment rate of two pence per pound of silver in 1637–38, Wollaston earned roughly £1,411 just from processing silver. This income placed him among the richest people in the kingdom. Meanwhile, in 1635, he secured, with seven other melters, the monopoly on supplying gold and silver to the gold and silver wire drawers. Wollaston had transformed himself from a fairly successful goldsmith to one of the richest and most successful goldsmiths—and indeed, merchants—in London.[4]

His wealth and social skills made him a natural for City of London politics. During the 1630s, he held positions in the city hierarchy that showed his growing influence. The two most important posts he filled were that of sheriff in 1636–37 and then alderman starting in 1639. Being an alderman was the more important position because it was akin to being a member of a city council in the United States today. The difference was that a man held the post of alderman for life. For nearly twenty years, until his death in 1658, Wollaston served as the City of London's alderman. The fact that Wollaston held a post in the City of London's government during the most tumultuous years in English history—when different factions controlled the city and Parliament—shows that he knew how to work with people, keep his mouth shut when necessary, and make and retain friends.

Wollaston's political skills were on display in the late 1630s and early 1640s. He and his wife, Rebecca, had Puritan sympathies but managed to stay on the right side of the king. For instance, he sponsored Puritan ministers in the 1630s—going so far as buying a parish and employing Puritan ministers there. In early modern England, the nine-thousand-odd parish churches had their own ministers, but a nobleman or a gentleman almost always owned the right to appoint the minister. The minister's position was called a living and dispensing these livings to family members or clients was a traditional means for the English elite to bestow patronage. Wollaston was rich enough to purchase a living in his home county of Staffordshire in 1630. He was committed enough to Puritanism that he gave the post to Ithiel Smart, a Presbyterian activist. Wollaston's Puritan tendencies meant that he did not approve of King Charles's efforts to reform the Church of England and, in 1639, when Charles demanded a loan from the aldermen of London to pay for his Scottish war, Wollaston declined to help his monarch. The next year, he refused to give a list of his wealthy neighbors to the king because the king wanted a "loan" from them as well.

One might think that this would have blacklisted Wollaston with the king. But in December 1641, Charles knighted him because Wollaston had signed a petition asking for a peaceful end to the intensifying conflict between Parliament and the king. That he managed to be knighted by a king with whom he disagreed on most political and religious issues is a testament to how well-liked and respected Wollaston was in London society. Charles may have hoped, too, that by knighting Wollaston he could secure his loyalty. However, Wollaston stayed true to his principles. When Charles fled London for Oxford in January 1642, Wollaston did not follow his king. Instead, he signed up to lead a militia regiment that helped keep the Royalists away from London. When the war started, he "became a major financier of the parliamentarian war effort, both advancing loans to parliament and administering its finances." Wollaston helped collect taxes for Parliament. He also served as the broker who sold Royalist lands during the war. He made such profit from land sales that he was able to afford £8,000 of his own money to purchase Royalist property north of London during the war.[5]

In 1643, Wollaston was elected Lord Mayor of London. From this lofty perch, he helped the war effort in every way possible. He began by eliminating his old nemesis Thomas Violet. Violet had caused Wollaston embarrassment and a great deal of money in 1636–37, when Violet accused Wollaston of illegally transporting gold and silver out of the country. Wollaston was never charged with any crime, but he had to give the king a gift in order to ensure no charges were brought against him and to protect his positions as the melter for the Royal Mint and the gold and silver wire drawers.

For Violet, the son of a Dutch musician, the older Wollaston seemed to have everything he wanted. Wollaston, like Violet, was childless and devoted to his work. Unlike Violet, though, he did not betray his fellow goldsmiths in order to make his fortune. Rather, Wollaston had earned his money by fortuitously attaining a key position in the money supply chain in London—a position that ensured him wealth and eventually political influence. In the late 1630s, Violet, always grasping to better himself at others' expense, may have thought that by damaging Wollaston, he could dismantle the goldsmiths' hierarchy and eventually acquire the lucrative positions Wollaston enjoyed. However, Violet's attack on Wollaston only earned him Wollaston's eternal enmity. Wollaston not only helped put Violet in prison in 1643, he also kept him there. During his incarceration in the Tower of London, Violet sent a petition to Parliament on May 19, 1646, begging to be released. The entry in the *Journal of the House of Commons* shows exactly how much anyone cared: "The humble Petition of Thomas Violett, Prisoner in the Tower, as this Day read; and nothing done upon it." Wollaston's political allies dominated Parliament at this point, and there was no way that Violet would even receive a hearing, let alone freedom. [6]

Violet had been as humiliated in every possible way by Wollaston. Further, with his connections and wealth, Wollaston seemed untouchable to Royalist Thomas Violet. Yet events in August and September 1647 gave Violet an opening against Wollaston. During those months, Parliament had debated and passed a law regulating clipped money. [7] Clipping money involved goldsmiths' shaving the edges off coins to store extra gold or silver for themselves. Before it passed the bill, Parliament brought all of the people involved in creating coinage to testify before the House of Commons. Their testimony terribly depressed the Members of Parliament because the witnesses admitted that everyone involved in the processing of gold and silver coins clipped money, including Wollaston himself.

From Wollaston's perspective, ironically, although he could make a fortune melting down large quantities of silver and gold, he was not compensated sufficiently for his work. He also may have felt justified clipping coins for extra money because he deserved it. He was almost single-handedly keeping the government functioning by helping supply the money the government used to pay its bills. In just one example, on October 7, 1647, Wollaston and several of his merchant colleagues lent Parliament £80,000 to keep the government running.[8] Of this, £32,000 was immediately sent to the army in the field to pay the noncommissioned troops.[9] The merchants would be paid back with interest by the government once monthly taxes came in. This transaction hints at why Parliament was willing to give Wollaston the benefit of the doubt when it came to lining his own pocket. As someone who kept Parliament's war machine running smoothly, he would not be discarded simply because he shaved some coins.

Wollaston, though, was not invincible. In 1649, Parliament reorganized the Royal Mint and fired all of the officers in the mint except for Wollaston. The Council of State then recommended that Wollaston become the next Master of the Mint. However, in a twist that no historian has yet been able to explain, the position of Master of the Mint went to Dr. Aaron Guerdain, a medical doctor, with an MA from Cambridge and an MD from Rheims, who did not appear to have any experience in the mint trade. He was simply a very well respected physician. Yet he received the position of Master of the Mint over Sir John Wollaston. Guerdain not only held the post, he continued his thriving medical practice in London. Why this happened no one knows for certain, but it may be that some Independents in Parliament did not want the Presbyterian Wollaston to control the mint.[10]

Although Wollaston was powerful and well connected, he did not get everything he wanted, which may have suggested to Violet that the time was right to attack him. During 1650–51, Violet devised a two-part plan to trap and discredit Wollaston. The first step was to present technical evidence proving Wollaston was hurting the English economy. The second was to smear him politically. Violet hoped that if one tactic did not work, the other would.

The first wave began in his late May 1650 petition to Parliament about trade and currency. Violet charged that "Mr. alderman [Wollaston] gives advice for the managing of a trade, and yet confesses it is a mystery beyond his understanding." Violet here accentuates his own expertise and erudition on the subject that Wollaston could not even understand, much less explain. Violet indicated that Wollaston not only did not deserve his lofty positions, he might not even comprehend why his actions were so awful for the English economy. Wollaston, was, in short, a liability to England.[11]

Then, in the summer of 1650, Violet wrote his pamphlet *A True Discovery to the Commons of England*, which explained how the goldsmiths were ruining the economy by exporting gold out of the country and wasting money by clipping it. According to Violet, the goldsmiths' illegal actions were bad for the economy. He noted that the 1647 act for regulating money required all English people to bring their clipped coins to goldsmiths who would in turn deliver them to the Royal Mint. The law obligated the mint pay the goldsmiths five shillings for every troy ounce of silver they furnished to the mint; however, they were actually charging the mint six shillings an ounce. [12] Further, the goldsmiths had found another way to cheat the mint: they only sent the mint money that had actually been clipped and kept the unclipped coins. Goldsmiths melted and shipped the heavy money out of the country to buy goods for English merchants. This collusion between the merchants and goldsmiths was draining England of precious metals and currency—exactly at a time it needed both. [13]

Violet's early arguments convinced the Council of State of the seriousness of this problem. Following his advice, the council proposed an act by which Violet would oversee the gold at the Royal Mint and send it to Parliament. As the executive body, the Council of State could send proposed legislation to the House of Commons. The House, though, had to pass it for the proposed act to become law. In this case, the Council of State recommended Violet's proposal to the House, a Member of Parliament introduced the bill, and on August 15, 1650, it was sent to a committee. There, in committee, the bill languished. It is not clear why this happened. It may be that in August 1650, the House was overwhelmed with the Scottish war and simply did not have time to take up financial reform. [14]

Violet continued his campaign. In November 1650, he petitioned Parliament to regulate the goldsmiths to protect English currency, and he did so again on January 1, 1651. Then, in February, at the request of John Bradshaw, president of the Council of State, Violet published his pamphlet on trade, *The Advancement of Merchandize*. In each of these cases, he explained that without solving the currency problem, the English Parliament would be hard pressed to pay its army and win its war against the Presbyterian Scots. In fact, it would help Parliament ensure that "the splendor and safety of the Commonwealth would [not] be undermined, which is the hearty desire of some of the Presbyterian party." [15] Wollaston's actions as melter, including clipping coins and sending money out of the country illegally, clearly revealed he was a type of Presbyterian that no one in the regime could, or should, trust. Since Violet had Bradshaw's backing in this endeavor, Wollaston and the goldsmiths were now targets of a powerful faction of the government. [16]

Having laid the groundwork that might weaken Wollaston in the Council of State's eyes, on June 2, 1651, Violet went in for the kill. He specifically explained how Wollaston's practices at the mint hurt England by describing to the Council of State how the Royal Mint used to work and how it was currently functioning. Before the 1620s, educated men operated the mint. They understood the technical aspects of melting precious metals and casting them into coins and also the record keeping necessary to keep track of the large amount of metal moving through the complex. This was no longer the case with Dr. Guerdain in charge and Wollaston circumventing him. The melter should not control the mint's production. In fact, being melter was so inconsequential that his salary was only supposed to be about £20 or £30 a year. Violet remarked that the position of melter was so unimportant that Wollaston never had to sign a contract with the state. Violet was correct—the records are not clear if Wollaston started working as a melter in 1624 or 1626.[17]

The real problem, according to Violet, was that, over the years, various English governments had hired men to oversee Wollaston, but they had not in fact understood what he was doing. Wollaston abused his trust when he melted down gold and silver by shaving sixteen "grains a lb. troy." These translated into a two pence profit over and above his actual payment for every three pounds of silver Wollaston processed. Violet claimed that Wollaston melted £900,000 worth of silver a year from 1630 through 1646. During that time, Wollaston earned £50,000 "for his waste in melting silver in the Mint." While Violet's numbers cannot be taken at face value, it appears that Violet was actually correct about the scope of the mint's production. After 1636–37, the mint produced more than £400,000 worth of silver in all but one year and during the war years even more: £825,707 in 1645–46 and £751,110 in 1646–47.[18] Violet's estimate rang true with the committee.

Violet made clear that if Wollaston had worked for men of less "ignorance or knavery," he would never have been able to take such a large sum from the country's treasury. What needed to happen instead, said Violet, was to place Violet himself in the position of master and melter of the mint. Violet explained that he could save the government 50 percent of its costs. He would take a smaller salary, £120 a year compared to Wollaston's £400 a year, and instead of wasting sixteen grains (a measurement of weight) for every pound of silver, he would only waste ten grains for every pound. This, Violet figured, would save "the State . . . by my discovery nearly 2,000£ a year."[19]

Violet then went on to explain what else he could do with the Royal Mint. One of its many problems was that its directors did not understand how money flowed in and out of the country. Currently, goldsmiths and merchants bought and sold foreign bullion to facilitate their own trade. It would be a very good thing for England if the person at the mint who was working with these merchants understood something about exchange rates. The current "warden, master worker, and comptroller are not skilled in holding intelligence from foreign parts concerning the bringing in of money." These men had admitted to Violet that he was the only person they had met who seemed to understand how international money markets worked. Not only that, Violet reported that "they found no man in London but myself that could understand every part of their business, to set them to rights, and show the way for regulating their fellowship of moneyers."[20]

He was so confident he understood everything about the money supply that Violet explained how he could save the government nearly £1,000 a year by simple administrative changes. According to Violet, it cost the Royal Mint £3,333 6s. 8d. to mint 100,000 pounds of silver. However, it only cost £2,400 "for workmen, coals, tools, and officers' fees," and that meant the state was overpaying by £930 every time it minted 100,000 pounds of coins. Even if his other plans did not save the government money, which they would, as soon as he was placed in charge and Wollaston was forced out, he would save the government a significant sum just by following protocol.[21]

Violet asked the Council of State to empower him to oversee the flow of money from goldsmiths to the Royal Mint, and subsequently in and out of the country. If he was allowed to do so, he promised that there would be less waste at the mint, that goldsmiths and merchants would not be allowed to ship precious metals out of the country illegally, and that when the English exchanged their coins for foreign currency, they would always get the better end of the deal. Further, he would oversee the mint's administration more efficiently than others had in the past and save the government a hefty sum by reducing overhead. And for all of this, all he wanted was that "they allow me one halfpenny the lb. weight out of their wages for all gold and silver they shall coin." This was one quarter of what Wollaston earned. In short, it was a financial windfall for the government.[22]

Violet was so close he could touch it. Wollaston would soon be gone and he would be the most important man in the Royal Mint, since Dr. Guerdain, the Master of the Mint, knew nothing about money. Yet his allies on the Council of State could not get Parliament to move on the matter. The likely reason was that during the years 1650 and 1651, the Independents in Parliament were by and large trying to reach out to their former allies, the Presbyterians, to widen the government's base of support. They were not going to destroy one of the most important Presbyterians in the city. Violet had, however, managed to attract the attention of the Council of State, which spoke to him repeatedly over a two-year period about these issues. Violet must have wrangled some sort of deal from the council, because they consulted him now on mint matters, instead of Wollaston or Guerdain. The records are not clear if, or how much, Violet was paid for this, but he was now involved at the highest level, and some in government no longer saw him as a Royalist.[23]

After December 1652, Violet's attention moved away from Wollaston and the Royal Mint to embark on what would be his most important contribution to the English government in his lifetime. Ironically, at nearly that same time, Wollaston would destroy himself because in May 1653 he finally made the wrong political move. From the summer of 1652 through the spring of 1653, Parliament and the army engaged in a drawn-out fight. By 1652, the army was no longer conquering any part of the British Isles, having occupied it all, but there was still a need for a very large army to subjugate Scotland and Ireland. There were several consequences of this situation. For the first time since the Norman Conquest in 1066, the English people had to pay high taxes for a standing army occupying parts of the British islands. One cost of these high taxes was Parliament's popularity—men did not enjoy giving the government a large percentage of their income year after year. Also, over the course of the Civil Wars and the conquest of Ireland and Scotland, the men in the army had developed close bonds—intellectual, religious, and political. They had come to believe that they were fighting for God's cause, and they wanted to turn England, and the rest of Britain, into a godly republic.

In a common failing of revolutionaries, they did not understand that their notion of the political and religious reforms most people desired was not in fact what the majority wanted. For instance, the army thought that individual parish churches' congregations should be independent and free to decide their theology. Most English people, though, thought that religion should be centrally organized in some way. Of course, Royalists wanted a hierarchical Church controlled by the king, and Presbyterians sought one controlled by the clergy; but both wanted central control. Since there were far more Royalists and Presbyterians combined in England than Independents, the army wanted nothing less than a religious transformation that would anger the vast majority of the country.

Political realities made their dream impossible to fulfill, and Parliament never passed any religious reform that suited the army. Many of the leaders of the army, especially the Lord General Oliver Cromwell, grew frustrated with Parliament. Then Parliament would not do something else the army wanted: hold elections. There had been no election for Parliament since the fall of 1640. The army believed that it had fought for a republic, so people should be able to vote for their representatives. However, again, the members of the army had spent too much time together on campaign and not enough time talking to ordinary English people. They did not realize that if there were free elections, the army's supporters would lose. The Members of Parliament knew this, but the leaders of the army just could not fathom it.

Both sides continued to get angrier at each other until Oliver Cromwell decided enough was enough. On April 19, 1653, he invited several Members of Parliament to his apartment in London and told them that the next day, Parliament needed to dissolve itself and that he and a small group of men would run the country until they decided how to set an election. Cromwell was so confident that Parliament would do this on April 20 that he did not dress to go out that day. Instead, he was shocked to hear that Parliament was debating a bill that would call for new elections—on its own terms, not his. Cromwell went to the House of Commons and sat down. (Cromwell was a Member of Parliament as well as a general.) He listened to the debates about the bill and then, just when the Speaker of the House was about to call for the vote, he stood up. He started calmly, but he got heated as he spoke. He put his hat on and began denouncing members by name as corrupt whoremasters who put the interests of the Presbyterians above the people. Finally, at the end of his speech, he yelled, "You are no parliament, I will put an end to your sitting." He then yelled, "Call them in! Call them in!"[24] A group of musketeers came into the chambers and then, calmly but forcibly, removed the members from the House. Oliver Cromwell and the army now ruled England.

Cromwell's actions spelled the end of Sir John Wollaston's political career. Wollaston opposed the military coup and in May 1653, along with other supporters of Parliament, petitioned Cromwell to restore Parliament. Wollaston's rebuff came quickly. On May 31, 1653, Cromwell fired him from his position as melter of the mint, a post he had held for nearly thirty years. Further, he lost his position as the nation's tax collector. While Wollaston would remain an alderman the rest of his life, because he was a Presbyterian who defied Cromwell, he lost. Thomas Violet, who had reminded anyone who would listen that Wollaston was a Presbyterian and an incompetent, was very pleased. His vengeance was nearly complete.[25]

NOTES

1. The *Oxford English Dictionary* spells the word "trepanner," using a 1659 example, while the pamphlet that called Violet that was published in 1660. Anon., *The Great Trappaner of England Discovered* (London, 1660).

2. *DNB*, vol. 59, 988.

3. Challis, "Lord Hastings to the Great Silver Recoinage, 1464–1699," 294–95, 311–12.

4. *DNB*, vol. 59, 988.

5. Ibid.

6. *CJ*, vol. 4, 550.

7. *CJ*, vol. 5, 284, 292.

8. *LJ*, vol. 9, 471–72.

9. *CSPD, 1645–47*, 573.

10. Challis, "Lord Hastings to the Great Silver Recoinage, 1464–1699," 325–26; *CSPD, 1649–50*, 129–30.

11. *CSPD, 1650*, 180, 181–82.

12. A troy ounce is slightly heavier than a regular ounce. Goldsmiths used it as a measurement of precious metals.

13. Violet, *A True Discovery to the Commons of England*, 46, 53–54.

14. *CJ*, vol. 6, 455.

15. Violet, *The Advancement of Merchandize*, 38.

16. *CSPD, 1650*, 431; Violet, *The Advancement of Merchandize*, 33–40.

17. Compare *DNB*, vol. 59, 988, with Challis, "Lord Hastings to the Great Silver Recoinage, 1464–1699," 294.

18. Challis, "Lord Hastings to the Great Silver Recoinage, 1464–1699," 313.

19. *CSPD, 1651*, 233.

20. Ibid.

21. Ibid., 234.

22. Ibid., 233.

23. *CSPD, 1651–52*, 156.

24. Woolrych, *Britain in Revolution*, quote 530; see 502–36 for a great summary and explanation of these events.

25. Challis, "Lord Hastings to the Great Silver Recoinage, 1464–1699," 294; *DNB*, vol. 59, 988.

Chapter Six

Republican

While Violet was lobbying the Council of State about John Wollaston, he adopted the habit of regularly attending the council meetings. Here he observed the central government's business as it developed day by day. Watching the Council of State in November 1652 drew Violet's attention away from Wollaston and toward an opportunity potentially far more profitable. What he would hear about, and then play a crucial role in, was a successful effort to acquire the majority of the silver bullion that the English government would mint into coins in the 1650s. Parliament, in part because of Violet's services, would impound three treasure ships, the *St. Salvador*, the *St. George*, and the *Samson*, over the winter and spring of 1652–53. Between them they carried silver worth more than £270,000. Since the Spanish source of English silver had dried up in 1648, this haul would be the largest single contributor to the English silver supply for the entire decade.[1] All of these efforts proved to the leaders of the government that Violet was no longer a Royalist but a supporter of the new republic. He was certainly Parliament's man now.

A combination of war with the Dutch, luck, and Violet's ability to understand and break down international shipping and smuggling information provided the opportunity for him. The war, called the First Anglo-Dutch War, was caused almost entirely by trade disputes. By 1651, everyone in England knew that the Dutch had not only cut off their supply of Spanish silver, but had also taken over most of Europe's bulk commodity shipping trade—all at England's expense. As noted in chapter 4, these events led the English Parliament to pass the Navigation Act on October 9, 1651, declaring that all goods shipped to England had to be transported either on an English ship or on a vessel from the merchant's country of origin. One aim of the act was to cut into the near-monopoly the Dutch held on international shipping. The Dutch ambassador knew that this act was aimed at his country's commercial interests, and he protested to the English government, but since he was a sophisticated politician, he did not push to escalate hostilities between the two nations. Many pro-Dutch Members of Parliament agreed; they did not want political conflict with the only other Protestant republic on earth. Over the winter and spring of 1651–52, the two governments worked toward a solution to the problem created by the Navigation Act and Dutch trade supremacy. [2]

While tensions between the two countries were high, clearly there were good reasons to keep the peace. However, in the spring of 1652, two developments caused the nations to go to war. The first was the press. An established press in both England and the Netherlands printed the news and commented on it. Neither country's press was free in the modern sense, but they were free to openly criticize foreigners. It was easy to do, rather fun, and sold weekly newsbooks. These were ubiquitous and over the course of 1652, nineteen different newsbooks appeared in England. [3] By this point in English history, virtually all literate people (about one third of the male population) read or were aware of the newsbooks. Thus, when the English newsbooks vilified the Dutch as enemies trying to destroy English prosperity, they helped fan anti-Dutch sentiment throughout England. [4]

While the press was whipping up xenophobia, captains on the high seas started an unofficial war. The English demanded that any ship in the English Channel strike its topsail when it approached an English naval vessel to show that it acknowledged their supremacy over "the British Sea." On May 19, 1652, a Dutch fleet of forty-two ships, led by fiercely anti-English admiral Martin Tromp, sailed past the English navy, which under the command of Robert Blake, who had fifteen ships in the English Channel. Blake told the Dutch to strike their topsails, and Tromp refused. Blake fired a few warning shots at the Dutch fleet to encourage Tromp to follow orders. Tromp responded by opening fire and a daylong battle ensued, resulting in the destruction of two Dutch ships. The press in both countries went berserk, each claiming that they were in the right and that they had to defend themselves against unprovoked attacks. The pro-Dutch faction in Parliament could not withstand the jingoism of the moment, and, by early summer, the two republics were at war. [5]

The English and Dutch navies engaged each other throughout western European waters. During the summer and fall, the fight was a draw. However, on December 10, 1652, the English fleet suffered a terrible defeat when Admiral Blake, with forty-five ships under his command, attacked Admiral Tromp and his eighty-five ships in the English Channel. Twenty of Blake's ships refused to fight, and Tromp sank two others. Blake had to retreat to Dover and cede control of the English Channel to the Dutch for the rest of the winter. Parliament responded by firing most of its captains and launching inquiries into the engagement. Things were so bad the government could not find any of its own captains willing to risk the Dutch blockade to sail to the Mediterranean to warn the English fleet and merchant marine there of the events of December 10. The only person who would risk running the Dutch gauntlet was Chris Shinner, a commander of a "Negro privateer."[6]

While news of naval defeats hurt English morale, the war also hit the English in their pocketbooks. Naval conflict was just as expensive, if not more so, than war on land. Financing the building, maintenance, crewing, and supply of the navy strained the country's budget. Almost as soon as the war started, Parliament began doing everything it could to pay for it. In December 1652, Parliament had to raise taxes to the Civil War height of £120,000 a month. The republic also accelerated its efforts to acquire and sell Royalist lands to help generate revenue. In November 1652, Parliament passed an act that took 678 estates from Royalists, which it immediately sold to generate income for the war effort.[7]

With the government so desperate for money, its leaders looked anywhere to raise revenue. One of the easiest ways was to capture Dutch merchant ships, sell their contents, and requisition the ships themselves for use in the English navy. English privateers (independent contractors hired as pirates) and Parliament's navy spread out over the North Sea, the Bay of Biscay, and the Mediterranean Sea in a quest for Dutch ships. Since the war was raging all over western European shipping lanes, the English plundering of merchant ships had a significant impact on merchants throughout Europe. The Dutch, of course, did the same, but because most European shipping was on Dutch vessels, raiding impacted the Dutch more. Consequently, Dutch merchants and their business partners in other countries started to devise ways to avoid English marauders. While they sometimes used convoys to fight the English off, they also tried another, cheaper, method of avoiding the English. They lied. They pretended to be anything other than Dutch. One simple way to dupe the English was to man their ships with international crews, which were easy to find in the sailing world.

They also altered their bills of lading—the official list of merchandise a ship had to carry. The bill was a combination of letters of introduction and safe passage, and a source of tax revenue. The contents of a ship had to match its bill to land at any reputable port. The Dutch fabricated the bills on their ships so that when English privateers captured them, they would raise the white flag, prove by their forged bill that they were a Spanish, German, or French ship, and then the English would have to let them go. The English understood what the Dutch were doing, and almost as a matter of course any merchant ship that fell into their net they escorted to Dover or to London. There, they would see if the bills onboard matched up to what was in the ship. Then, if there were discrepancies, particularly if a ship turned out to be Dutch, they would seize the ship. [8]

This was the fate of the three ships caught by the English navy in November 1652. The first two, the *St. Salvador* and the *St. George*, hailed from Hamburg, and the third, the *Samson*, came from Lubeck. All three set sail from the Spanish port of Cadiz on October 13, 1652. Their final port of call in Spain was just a few miles away from Cadiz, the little port of Sanlucar, the central location of Spanish smuggling. According to Violet, beyond the sandbar at Sanlucar, foreign ships lay in wait for the Spanish treasure fleet. There, they illegally picked up Spanish silver and transported it to different ports in Europe. [9]

Further, the allegedly German-owned ships, the *St. Salvador*, the *St. George*, and the *Samson*, were, in fact, controlled by Dutch merchants, who were moving Spanish silver into the Netherlands for their own purposes. They hid the silver by packing the ships with tobacco and Spanish wool. Both were legitimate exports to the Netherlands where men smoked and weavers processed Spanish wool in great quantities. While the Dutch hoped that the tobacco and wool would hide the silver from any inspectors, they had another plan in case that failed. They kept in contact with a wide range of English merchants. Even during the war, English and Dutch merchants transacted business with each other. Trade had to be done illegally in wartime, with both sides using elaborate ruses to prove to the authorities that they were not trading with the enemy. While in the case of the *St. Salvador*, the *St. George*, and the *Samson*, the Dutch were not working to illegally smuggle goods into and out of England, their prior efforts did mean that they had contacts with several key London-based merchants, particularly James Sten-eer, also known as Jacomo Staneir. [10]

The ships left Spain and set sail for the Netherlands. On the way they landed in Calais, France, and then moved north. They never made it to Amsterdam. Rather, they were captured by an Englishman, Captain Rey-nolds, who brought them to Tilbury Hope, a small town on the Thames River across from Gravesend, one of the last stops before the Thames flows into the English Channel. News of the ships' capture came to London by November 11, maybe November 12. Over the course of November 12, the Council of State received an evolving picture of the ships and the contents of their holds. As a matter of course, once a captured ship was brought into English waters, it was placed under the jurisdiction of Dr. Walter Walker, the judge advocate for the Admiralty Court. [11] Walker would investigate whether a putative Dutch ship was in fact a Dutch ship, and hence could be impounded, or a neutral ship that would have to be let go. If Walker believed it was a Dutch vessel, he brought his case before the Admiralty Court. If the court agreed that it was a Dutch ship, then the Commission for Prize Goods inventoried the goods on the ship for either immediate use, or sold them at Parliament's discretion.

Early in the day on November 12, the council informed Walker and the Admiralty judges that ships claiming to hail from Hamburg had come in. The councilmen wanted them investigated and ordered Walker to have his pre-liminary report on the ships available by the next morning at 8 a.m. Mean-while, Captain Reynolds had clearly inventoried the ships, because the Coun-cil of State knew that there was a potential fortune inside. Later in the day, it ordered the Commissioners of Dutch Prize Goods to keep all of the goods onboard the ships so that "there would be no embezzlement." [12] News of the ships' capture and their rich cargo spread quickly throughout London. That evening the Spanish ambassador stormed into the council chambers and de-manded that the ships be released. He argued that they were Hamburg-based ships legally transporting goods from Spain and should not be molested. Further, if in fact they were illegally transporting Spanish silver, that silver would belong to the Spanish government, not to the English. [13]

James Steneer, the Dutch agent who worked as a merchant in London, quickly wrote several letters to Antwerp, warning his Dutch business part-ners that the Commonwealth of England had captured their silver and that the Spanish ambassador was angling for it. Unfortunately for Steneer, his letters were intercepted by the English government's intelligence services on November 19. These took a few days to move through channels, but it soon became clear from the letters that Steneer was going to try to bribe some "great ones" in the English government to get the silver released to its alleged Hamburg-based owner. On December 1, 1652, the House of Commons called Steneer in to explain himself. He said that the "great ones" mentioned in his letters were not meant to be Englishmen but rather the Spanish ambassador and his secretary, who Steneer claimed needed to be bribed so that the Hamburg-based merchants could recover their silver.[14]

Walker, the judge advocate responsible for investigating the ships' legality and country of origin, faced a potential international incident. He was also incredibly busy because on November 18 he had fourteen captured "Hamburg" ships to investigate, a number that reached twenty by November 22. By this point, Walker found himself in a firestorm of petitions and counterpetitions; merchants from Hamburg complained that the English had illegally captured their vessels. Meanwhile, English merchants would either claim that the prizes should be seized and sold (to them, below market value) or that they were legitimate traders and should be sent on their way. If that was the case, the factors, or owners, of the goods might be expected to offer a gratuity to the English merchants for their help. This last development led to rumors that Walker might be releasing some ships he thought were Hamburg-owned ships but which were actually Dutch owned.[15]

Walker was overwhelmed and under tremendous pressure when, on December 3, the Council of State asked him for an update on the case of the *Samson*, the *St. Salvador*, and the *St. George*. At some point during that week, Walker probably decided that there was not enough evidence to prove that the three ships were Dutch. While not pleased with this finding, but facing pressure from the Spanish ambassador, the Council of State ordered Walker to move forward with his case in the Admiralty Court on December 6.

Violet chose this moment to strike. Violet, a regular at the meetings of the Council of State and Parliament, had observed the case of the silver ships with interest. Further, in recent weeks, Violet had attended the meetings of the Admiralty Court and watched how the three judges interacted with various merchants after court was out of session. He realized that the judges were being bribed by businessmen with Dutch connections. Violet knew from his own experience what was going on. Dutch merchants controlled the silver. Not wanting to lose a fortune in silver, they used their English friends to manipulate the legal process so that the three ships would be declared Hamburg ships and hence free to go. The Dutch merchants hired members of the Dutch crew to steal some of the silver off the ships, and take it to an English business partner, who used it to bribe the judges. At the same time, the Spanish ambassador pursued his own course by trying to get the English legal system to rule that the silver was being exported illegally from Spain, which would force the court to decide in his favor and return the silver to Spain.[16]

On December 7, Violet asked the Council of State if he could present evidence on the matter to the Committee on Foreign Affairs, the body that oversaw the Admiralty Court, the next day. His testimony caught the committee's attention. He informed them that the silver in the holds of the *Samson*, the *St. Salvador*, and the *St. George* did not belong to German-speaking merchants. Rather, it belonged to Dutch merchants. While this might be something that many of the men on the committee wanted to hear, Violet had to be able to prove his allegations. Violet's telling them that it was Dutch silver meant nothing unless he could prove it—which he eagerly did. He explained that the judges at the Admiralty Court were deliberately dragging their feet when investigating the case of the three ships. While they did so, merchants in London and overseas were writing "counterfeit Bills of lading." Violet told the committee, "I have good reason to believe the hearts, purses, heads, and books of accounts of many Merchants of London, will be all ready to assist the Dutch-Merchants to cozen the State of this Treasure." As Violet reminded the committee, since he had "formerly been privy to the proceedings of Merchants that have transported gold and silver out of this Nation, and also acquainted with several Merchants that have yearly imported silver from Spain," he understood how merchants worked together to deceive or bribe government officials to cheat the state out of its rightful prizes.[17]

Violet warned the committee that Walker was going to make a terrible mistake if he did not understand this. Convinced that Violet knew what he was talking about, the Council of State ordered Violet to "assist, on behalf of the commonwealth, in the prosecution of the suits now in the Court of Admiralty against the *Samson*, *Salvador*, and *George*, and to acquaint Dr. Walker from time to time with what he has to offer in reference to them."[18] However, the council also informed Violet that he could not do this as an official agent of the council. If it paid him a salary to prove that the Spanish government did not have a claim on the silver, that might spark a war with Spain—a war the government could ill afford when it was already hard-pressed to fight the

Dutch. Violet agreed. He said that he wanted only his fair share of the prize—maybe £11,000 of the first £100,000 of silver the government collected. According to Violet, the council assented. Violet immediately started collecting information from his contacts on the wharves and in the merchant community about the ships. He was on good terms with Mr. Watkins, the head of the port of London, and Watkins kept Violet informed of the gossip at the port. Violet heard troubling rumors. Otho George, captain of the *Samson*, was collecting provisions onboard his ship for a voyage because he knew that the judges of the Admiralty would release his ships at their next meeting on December 16.[19]

During the week of December 8–15 Violet hired "several men who spake [*sic*] the Dutch Language . . . and gave them money to go on ship board, and to drink freely with the Dutch mariners, and in their cups to fish out the secrets of this business." Violet bought his spies "Brandy-wine, strong beer, rum, and Spruce beer, pickle Herrings and Holland cheese" to share with the Dutch crew. From them, he confirmed that the ship was laden with Dutch silver. Further, he recognized that when Walker had taken testimony from the passengers onboard the ships, they had all lied about their country of origin. Armed with this knowledge, Violet tried to find all of the passengers but found it difficult because they "were . . . packed away by the Claimers . . . and had money given them that they should keep out of the way." Not only were the passengers being bribed to stay away and stay silent, Violet also heard that "Spanish Gold and Silver was plentifully bestowed on some in the Admiralty, and they loved it well."[20]

While Violet was collecting information, the Dutch merchants were moving in the Court of the Admiralty. They bribed two of the three judges and were confident that the ships would be freed after the 9 a.m. meeting of the Court of the Admiralty on December 16. Otho George knew the merchants had bought the court and prepared the *Samson* to sail. It also meant that Steneer's confederates, if not the man himself, were doing a fine job manipulating events to their liking. Meanwhile, on December 14, the Spanish ambassador went to the House of Commons and demanded to be heard. Violet briefly hoped that this would put pressure on the bribed judges and halt the proceedings, but he quickly saw it would not. Violet realized that if the bribed judges at the Admiralty Court let the ships go and if Violet did not stop it, on December 16 the boats would be freed. Already supplied, they would slip away and never return. On the fifteenth, Violet reported these concerns to the Council of State. Once again, the leaders of the council told him they could not endorse his actions, fearing a rift with Spain. However, he, on his own, could denounce the judges and stop the proceedings at the court by making his allegations and evidence known. On the morning of December 16, the Court of Admiralty met to decide the fate of the three ships. The judges were about to agree that the silver belonged to the original (i.e., Dutch) merchants when Violet strode into the court. He told them that they could not go forward with the "discharge [of] this silver in the aforesaid ships." They would have to listen to his witnesses first, who would prove that their current judgment would hurt the Commonwealth. [21]

The judges adjourned the court until the next day. Violet remembered "the judges being very angry with" him and that they ordered him to attend a meeting of the Council of State that afternoon to justify his outlandish accusations. Claiming that judges of the Court of Admiralty were hurting the Commonwealth in this time of war was not something one did lightly. Yet Violet confidently explained to the Council of State and the judges that both the Dutch and the Spanish wanted the silver and that the Admiralty Court was about to give it to them. He could not have picked a better time to make this case in front of the council. During the worst month of the war, with taxes just raised to record highs, and with a silver shortage, Thomas Violet was telling the most powerful men in the land, including his patron John Bradshaw, president of the council, that he could legally prove that hundreds of thousands of pounds of free money had just landed in their laps. The council instructed the judges to listen to Violet and his evidence. [22]

Violet set out to prove that widespread corruption in the Court of Admiralty had cost England a fortune already in the war and would cost it even more in the future. Violet revealed that from August until December 1652, the Commonwealth had captured fifty-eight ships, "all laden with rich merchandize" that it had discharged. These ships were let go by the Admiralty Court because they demonstrated they were neutral ships. But Violet could prove through a series of witnesses and forged letters that these ships in fact, once they were freed, "unloaded their merchandize at Amsterdam for the account of the Dutch." He declared that the cargoes of these ships were worth "many hundred thousand pounds." The Court of Admiralty let the ships go because the merchants who owned the merchandise bribed members of the court. The members were earning up to £5,000 a year to look the other way while Dutch shipping disappeared from London. [23] To top it off, on December 16, while he was leveling these charges at the court before the Council of

State, he claimed that the Admiralty was preparing to discharge seventeen held ships that carried 3,400 tons of cargo.[24]

Violet's accusations caused a sensation and immediate counteraccusations. By this point, Violet was a well-known presence around the Council of State and men knew him as a former Royalist notorious for devious plots all too often designed only to enrich himself. The merchants responsible for the bribes came forward with this very information. Meanwhile, pro-Dutch Members of Parliament were aghast at what he was saying and wanted him silenced. Further, the Presbyterians who had joined the government again would have liked nothing better than to throw him back in the Tower of London for his slander of them in 1650–51. Finally, poor Dr. Walker was not up to the task of being the judge advocate to help Violet in his cause. Walker told Violet that he should relent and forget the whole thing.[25]

Walker had good reason to be afraid because some members of the Council of State were so angry about Violet's actions that they were ready to do him harm. Violet heard that some members wanted to "hang me for staying this Silver." The only reason Violet was not ignored was John Bradshaw was still the president of the Council of State and he and other anti-Dutch politicians provided Violet political cover for his acts. Bradshaw, by all accounts, was an honorable man, so it is hard to understand what he saw in Violet. But Violet had managed, from 1650 through 1652, to convince Bradshaw that he understood international trade and that his actions could bring hundreds of thousands of pounds of income to the cash-strapped Commonwealth.[26]

Violet had argued his case well by stating the simple truth that the King of Spain had not registered the silver. The bill of trade clearly proved it. If the Spanish had registered the silver, then they would have legally owned it. Further, if Spanish ships had captured the *St. Salvador*, the *St. George*, and the *Samson*, the Spanish government would have been free to impound the ships. However, the Spanish navy had not captured the treasure ships; rather, the English had. So the King of Spain had no legal claim on the silver because he could not prove it was his. Violet also revealed that Dutch merchants who actually were controlling the silver were so good at forging documents that in no time at all they would bring counterfeit documents that would prove that the silver belonged to the King of Spain. These forged documents would allow them to take the treasure ships "back" to Spain. Instead of Spain, though, they would of course bring the silver to Amsterdam. Even if they could not return the silver to Holland, they would be much happier with the silver going to Spain or even Hamburg rather than staying with the English whom they were currently fighting.[27]

Over the months of December 1652 and January 1653, Violet worked tirelessly to prove that the silver in the ships could be impounded. He hired people to collect information from crew members, merchants, and government employees. He presented any piece of evidence, no matter how unlikely, that proved the silver belonged to the Dutch. The Committee on Foreign Affairs took his reports seriously even when they sounded outlandish. On January 4, 1653, Violet excitedly reported the following information to the council: he had spoken to a Sir Sackville Crowe in Whitehall about the silver ships. Whitehall at that time was the palace that was the seat of the English government. Sir Sackville told Violet that he had an acquaintance named Pompey Calendrine, Philip Burlamacke's brother-in-law. Burlamacke worked as a bookkeeper in the Royal Mint. Pompey had told Sir Sackville that Philip told him that Burlamacke reported that the silver was Dutch. While his information may have been hearsay, Violet brought Pompey's and Sir Sackville's testimony to the Committee on Foreign Affairs, whose members eagerly listened to it.[28]

The cumulative impact of Violet's evidence convinced the Committee on Foreign Affairs that the *St. Salvador*, the *St. George*, and the *Samson* were, in fact, Dutch ships that could be impounded. However, because there was so much silver onboard the ships, the various other claimants, including the merchants who bribed the judges at the Admiralty Court, continued to resist the charges. Over the winter and spring, the Commonwealth responded to numerous inquiries from merchants from Hamburg, the Spanish government, and Lubeck. The government also constantly directed its agents to guard the treasure ships more carefully because it feared that men were stealing the silver. Further, the men onboard the ships were getting more and more desperate. The surgeon onboard the *Samson* decided to testify that it was a Dutch ship. In retaliation, Otho George, the captain, attacked him. George also knew that Violet was behind the effort to impound his silver and he told everyone he met that he would kill Violet, if he could find him. Violet took George's threat seriously and spent a week at home in the middle of March to avoid him.[29]

Yet, by early April 1653, it appeared that even the Spanish had given up trying to claim the silver. On April 8, Spanish merchants asked about the tobacco onboard the ship, tacitly acknowledging that they no longer had a case for the silver.[30] Then, on April 20, Oliver Cromwell threw out the

Members of Parliament and installed himself and a few other key allies as the provisional rulers of England. Just two weeks later, the case finally broke open. On May 4, 1653, the Commissioners of Prize Goods reported to Cromwell and his provisional Council of State that Otho George had made the purser (recordkeeper) of the three ships "alter his book, taking out the names of all Hollanders and Zealanders, and inserting others." Then, the purser of the ships had thrown "their letters overboard tied to an iron bar, on coming into the Downs." The pro-Dutch English merchants and the crew then "attack[ed] the surgeon and others who could bear evidence against them." Next, information from France revealed that when these ships docked in Calais, the crews told everyone that they were from Amsterdam. However, once they saw the English, they said that they were from Ostend (a port city in modern-day Belgium). Finally these men "altered their bills of lading, and tried to hide the silver." In order to confuse the English authorities, they "Pretend to be Hamburghers." They were found out, though, because they "Only [spoke] low Dutch."[31]

Cromwell decided it was now time to coin the silver, because a few days later, under heavy guard, troops transported the silver from the ships to the Royal Mint. On May 16, one of Cromwell's key supporters, General Thomas Harrison, asked Sir John Wollaston to oversee the melting of the silver before it was cast into coins. Wollaston thought that because the new government trusted him with the silver that he had enough influence with Cromwell to petition Cromwell to bring back Parliament. Wollaston had seriously miscalculated, though, because Cromwell not only ignored the petition but also stripped Wollaston of his position as melter of the mint. Violet took advantage of Wollaston's fall to inform Cromwell's council that someone might steal the silver. The council responded by ordering all of the keys to the room in the Tower of London where the silver was held be taken into custody. At this point, Cromwell's two top lieutenants, Generals Harrison and John Lambert, both said that Thomas Violet should be responsible for overseeing the investigation of the possible embezzlement of the state's silver. Violet was flying high. The leaders of a military coup thought that he was the man who earned a fortune with promises of discovering much more. It is clear why they believed him. After all, everything he had said was right about the *St. Salvador*, the *St. George*, and the *Samson*.[32] The amount of silver recovered from the silver ships was astonishing. The final value of these ships (along with two others) was £276,702. Of this, £239,560 went directly into the navy's budget—a significant and important contribution to the war effort.

Everyone Violet spoke to acknowledged that the silver was crucial and many recognized that he had played a key role in proving that the government could impound the ships.[33]

There was only one rather significant problem for Violet in all of this. He needed to be rewarded for all of his work. Violet did not have a steady source of income and, in fact, had to borrow money to run his investigation. He figured that he borrowed £765 to pay for all of his spies, not to mention the beer that he purchased to prove that the silver belonged to England. Yet Violet did not just want £765 in expenses as his reward. He wanted returned to him the entire value of his estate that he had lost during the Civil War. During the war, he had valued his total net worth at about £8,400. In the ensuing years, Violet had decided that his pre–Civil War net worth was actually £11,000. He repeatedly claimed that the Council of State had told him in December 1652 that if he managed to get the Spanish silver, the council would return his entire estate.

Violet's wealth had come from several sources. He had held the bonds on two estates. He had owned several paper bonds, worth £2,000. He had controlled the lease on rental property in London, and he had overseen the gold and silver wire drawers. Violet wanted all of that returned to him, but three major obstacles blocked him. First, he did not have a written agreement with the Council of State, so the government was under no legal obligation to pay him. Second, he was demanding a small fortune from a cash-strapped government that would have to deprive people of their property to compensate him. Finally, the government he had worked for in the winter of 1652–53 had ceased to exist on April 20, 1653. While Violet quickly went about working for the new regime and making close connections with the leading generals in Cromwell's government, he had no legal case to make for his pay. Yet he remained confident he would earn most, if not all, of his estate back. After all, it had taken him several years to convince Charles I to appoint him overseer of the gold and silver wire drawers, and it might take months to convince Cromwell that he deserved his reward.

Oliver Cromwell had more important problems than paying Thomas Violet. Now that he had expelled Parliament, Cromwell needed to create a working English government. During 1653, Cromwell experimented with several types of government. He and the Council of State ruled directly for a few months before they brought in a Parliament of godly men. These men were not elected by the people but rather nominated by the army's Council of Officers. Cromwell's goal was to bring in very religious men who would serve for a brief time, set the country to rights, and dissolve themselves so the country could have free elections. The Nominated Assembly, its legal title, quickly became known as the Barebones' Parliament, after one of its members, Praise God Barebones. These religious zealots proved unequal to the task of running the country, and Cromwell dissolved the asembly that winter. On December 16, 1653, Cromwell took the title of Lord Protector, a position he would hold for the rest of his life. For the next five years, Cromwell was king in all but name, and while he tried different sorts of Parliaments during this time, he stood as the center of English government.[34]

As the months went by, Violet clearly recognized that Oliver Cromwell was the person he needed to convince that he deserved his £11,000. He started working on Cromwell's subordinates almost immediately. On April 27, he sent a letter to General Monk, Cromwell's admiral at the time. On May 4, Violet petitioned the new Council of State. On May 24, he delivered a packet of information to the council explaining what he had done. On June 21, he sent another letter to the council. Finally, on August 3, 1653, Violet paid for a pamphlet called *A True Narrative of som remarkable-Procedings* [*sic*], in which he summarized his efforts for the English government over the previous ten months.[35] Nothing came of these petitions. However, during the interim, there were more claims against the silver ships that the Council of State had to fend off. In September 1653, the Council of State asked Violet to help them disprove a £20,000 claim by George Boschaert for a share of the silver as well as verify the veracity of his witnesses. Violet agreed to do so (proving it in the negative) and by October 1653, the council had made it official that Violet was to represent it when someone challenged the legality of the government's actions.[36]

After working for Cromwell's government for months Violet had high hopes in February 1654 that it would respond to his petition to pay him for services rendered. The Council of State took him seriously. It created a subcommittee to look into his billing in a no doubt legitimate desire to pay him for his work.[37] However, the demands on the state's funds continued unabated, and there simply was no money to compensate Violet. Then in March 1656, Violet spoke with John Corbet, a Member of Parliament. Corbet told Violet that his three bonds worth £2,000 were currently held by the town of Shrewsbury in Shropshire, Corbet's home. This was news to Violet. At the moment, the bonds were mortgaged for £40, which meant that anyone who paid the £40 would control the £2,000 worth of bonds. Bonds in the 1650s were not like modern government bonds. Rather, they were more like promissory notes individuals took out and promised to pay. Since the mortgage on the £2,000 in bonds was only £40, this suggests that virtually no one in Shropshire thought the bonds could ever be redeemed for their full value. However, Thomas Violet knew the men who issued the bonds and he believed that he could collect on them. Corbet suggested that Violet redeem the bonds for £40 himself and thus receive a major down payment on the money he claimed was owed to him. Corbet's plan had the added bonus of costing the government nothing. Happy to help Violet at no cost, on March 21, 1656, Cromwell and his council ordered "the Committee of Salop" to sell their bond to Violet.[38]

As far as Cromwell's government was concerned, the matter was settled. During the Civil Wars, the government had often paid people less than they demanded for services rendered, and £2,000 was a substantial sum. However, Violet had a legal problem. Since his estates were sequestered during the Civil Wars, he no longer had a legal claim to them. Ultimately, the bonds were part of his estate, so he needed Parliament to act to reverse the sequester of his estate. As long as Parliament did not do this, the men who owed him money on the bonds had no legal obligation to pay him even though he had the bonds in his possession. Further, he felt he was owed the rest of his £11,000, so he continued to lobby the government for a better settlement.[39]

In 1657, Violet tried another big push to get the whole thing settled. This time, he even managed to get John Bradshaw, the former president of the Council of State, to say that Violet was the key player in securing the silver ships. Although the events in question had occurred almost five years earlier at this point, Bradshaw wrote that Violet provided critical evidence to impound the ships and that there had been a verbal agreement with him that he would be paid. Bradshaw did admit that he could not verify all of the exact claims Violet made, particularly regarding recompense, but that Violet did deserve something. By 1658, all this effort began to pay off. On May 1, Cromwell told his council to look into paying Violet for his efforts. On July 29, Violet reminded Cromwell that the committee was supposed to examine his affairs and Cromwell again reminded the committee to look into paying him. But Cromwell died on September 3, 1658, before his committee could report to him, stalling Violet's effort.[40]

Violet did not give up, though. Cromwell's son Richard Cromwell succeeded him as Lord Protector and Violet immediately began petitioning Richard for his money. In October, Richard asked two men to look into Violet's affairs, and on January 19, 1659, reported that Violet should be paid

£765 for his expenses as well as the position of overseer of the gold and silver wire drawers. Unfortunately for Violet, Richard Cromwell was not up to the challenge of running the country, and in the spring of 1659 the army dissolved Richard's Parliament and retired him. The army then called back the Parliament expelled by Oliver Cromwell on April 20, 1653. This Parliament, called the Rump Parliament, lasted until October, when the army dissolved it again for interfering in its affairs. The army tried to rule directly for two months but could not manage so the generals invited the Rump Parliament back again. The government was clearly falling apart. Amid the turmoil, in the spring of 1659, Violet actually petitioned the Rump Parliament for his money, but it had more pressing worries than the now six-year-old concerns of one goldsmith. Violet was coming to the conclusion he would never get his money.[41]

Violet faced ruin because he had not earned any money during the entire decade. Rather, he had been living off loans from acquaintances and business associates who lent him money on the promise he would pay them back once he was reimbursed by the government. He had borrowed money from the goldsmith Alexander Holt and the printer William Dugard. Dugard, like Violet, was a Royalist who started working for the Commonwealth in the 1650s because he had no other option. By the spring of 1659, Violet had borrowed £1,500 from these men and others to keep himself in bread over the course of the decade. That, combined with the £765 he borrowed during the investigation in 1652–53, meant that Violet owed more than he was worth—£2,000 in bonds he could not cash. As the years went on, Violet grew embittered. He felt the government had strung him along with promises to pay him his money, promises that never materialized. Many times, he felt he had achieved his goal only to have it snatched away. He might have also practiced a little self-deception, as he would "remember" that several years before someone had promised to ensure that the government paid him when, in fact, they had only promised to look into his account. In any event, as the chaotic year 1659 followed its uncertain course, Violet realized he would never get out of debt if he did not try something else. As he told his creditors in 1659, he would hate to "be made an instrument to Trappan you or . . . to cozen you of your money."[42] So instead of trying to get any more money from the state, Violet decided a new course. It was time to take aim at a wealthy group that no one liked and that had no legal protection—the Jews.

NOTES

1. Challis, "Lord Hastings to the Great Silver Recoinage," 322; Thomas Violet, *A True Narrative of the Proceedings in the Court of Admiraltie* (London, 1659), title page.

2. Woolrych, *Britain in Revolution*, 507–12.

3. *English Short Title Catalog (ESTC)*, ESTC Online, accessed October 14, 2014, http://estc.bl.uk/F/?func=file&file_name=login-bl-estc.

4. Braddick, *God's Fury, England's Fire*, 50.

5. Woolrych, *Britain in Revolution*, 511–12.

6. *CSPD, 1652–53*, 48.

7. Woolrych, *Britain in Revolution*, 512–14; *CSPD, 1652–53*, 11, 171.

8. Thomas Violet, *A True Narrative of som remarkable-Procedings concerning the ships Samson, Salvadore and George* (London, 1653), 14–15.

9. *CSPD, 1651–52*, 489–90; Violet, *A True Narrative of som remarkable-Procedings*, 8, 27. On page 8 Violet says the ships' last port in Spain was Sanlucar; on page 27 he says it was Cadiz.

10. *CSPD, 1652–53*, 266, 305; *CJ*, vol. 7, 223–24; Violet. *A True Narrative of the Proceedings in the Court of Admiraltie*, 122–23.

11. The primary sources use a variety of names for the same court or the same commission. The name used in any instance in this text reflects the name as spelled in the source.

12. *CSPD, 1651–52*, 490.

13. Ibid., 489–92.

14. *CJ*, vol. 7, 223–24.

15. *CSPD, 1651–52*, 498, 501, 504, 505, 506, 509.

16. *CSPD, 1652–53*, 7, 11, 40; Violet, *A True Narrative of the Proceedings in the Court of Admiraltie*, 4–5, 9, 71.

17. Violet, *A True Narrative of som remarkable-Procedings*, 6–7.

18. *CSPD, 1652–53*, 23.

19. Violet, *A True Narrative of the Proceedings in the Court of Admiraltie*, 4, 84, 125.

20. Ibid., 70–71.

21. Ibid., 4, 80–82, 124–25; Violet, *A True Narrative of som remarkable-Procedings*, 17.

22. Violet, *A True Narrative of the Proceedings in the Court of Admiraltie*, 4–5.

23. Ibid., 7–8.

24. Violet, *A True Narrative of som remarkable-Procedings*, sig. Br.

25. Ibid., sig. B2r, unpaginated; some of the pages are not numbered because of a printer's error; Violet, *A True Narrative of the Proceedings in the Court of Admiraltie*, 71.

26. Violet, *A True Narrative of som remarkable-Procedings*, sig. Cv–C2v, unpaginated.

27. Ibid., 11–12.

28. Ibid., 31–32, *CSPD, 1652–53*, 75.

29. Violet, *A True Narrative of the Proceedings in the Court of Admiraltie*, 4, 67; *CSPD, 1652–53*, 98, 128, 129, 137, 171, 198, 241, 245, 266; Violet, *A True Narrative of Som remarkable Proceedings*, 48.

30. *CSPD, 1652–53*, 266.

31. *CSPD, 1652–53*, 305, for quotations. For Violet's view, see Violet, *A True Narrative of som remarkable-Procedings*, 10.

32. *CSPD, 1652–53*, 330, 371, 393, 395, 398.

33. *CSPD, 1654*, 336; Violet, *A True Narrative of the Proceedings in the Court of Admiraltie*, 77.

34. Woolrych, *Britain in Revolution*, 537–40, 563.

35. Violet, *A True Narrative of som remarkable-Procedings*, sig. Dr, 73–93.

36. *CSPD, 1653–54*, 123, 152, 162, 178, 199.

37. Ibid., 412.

38. Violet, *A True Narrative of the Proceedings in the Court of Admiraltie*, 45–49; *CSPD, 1655–56*, 117, 129, 235. The "Committee of Salop" was the local government body overseeing Salop.

39. Violet, *A True Narrative of the Proceedings in the Court of Admiraltie*, 49–50.

40. Ibid., 80–82, 22.

41. Ibid., 111–12, 114–17, 148. BL Harley MS 6034 passim; Bucholz and Key, *Early Modern England 1485–1714*, 274.

42. For Dugard, see Amos Tubb, "Independent Presses: The Politics of Print in England During the late 1640s," *Seventeenth Century* 27, no. 3 (Autumn 2012): 293; Violet, *A True Narrative of the Proceedings in the Court of Admiraltie*, 122, quote 134.

Chapter Seven

Anti-Semite

Violet's decision to attack the Jews of London stemmed from his need for money and his hatred and envy of his neighbor Antonio Carvajal. He devised a plot where he would use the Jews to secure a position at the Royal Mint. Violet had tried for years to find a post there. During the 1650s, he wrote several long pamphlets to Oliver Cromwell explaining how the gold and silver supply really worked, the role of coins in the economy, and how he could make the mint run more efficiently, if he had a position of authority there. He also explained that he could manufacture counterfeit-proof coins. Violet never secured a position because Cromwell decided to employ a Frenchman at the mint, Pierre Blondeau, who actually made counterfeit-proof coins. Blondeau's radical idea to prevent counterfeiting was to use a machine that placed ridges on both sides of the outside rim of each coin, which made it obvious for anyone to see if they had been clipped. This dramatic new idea won Cromwell over, and the coins Blondeau made for Cromwell were a major innovation that would be adopted by later English governments. Throughout Cromwell's reign, Violet strove to prove he would be a better choice for melting at the mint, but to no avail. Cromwell stuck with Blondeau and his counterfeit-proof coins. [1]

However, once Oliver Cromwell died and Richard Cromwell came to power, Violet imagined that he had another chance to find a place at the Royal Mint. He hoped to be the melting houses' surveyor, the person who enforced the government's edicts to prevent the production of counterfeit coins. The man who held the post, Richard Pight, had spent the 1650s hunting down false coiners—finding eighty-six between 1650 and 1659. Violet knew that in order to get Pight's position, he would have to prove that Pight himself was responsible for minting and selling counterfeit coins. Pight was almost certainly already doing this—the key would be for Violet to provide irrefutable proof that Pight was doing so.[2]

In the winter of 1658–59, Violet set in motion a plot that would expose Pight to discredit him and take his job. The plan involved getting Pight to participate in the illegal production of foreign coins. Violet would trick Pight into approving the manufacture of a large quantity of counterfeit foreign coins that he would sell to the Jews of London. These Jews, who had many foreign connections, would then sell the coins overseas. The two-part plan ensured that Violet not only discredited Pight but also implicated the Jews, which would make them liable for criminal fines that Violet hoped to collect. The Jews were tempting targets for Violet because in 1659, Jews had only lived quasi-legally in England for three years, having been expelled from the country in 1290. The banishment meant that the vast majority of English people had had virtually no regular contact with Jews for about three and a half centuries. Consequently, English views of Jews were entirely created by European popular culture, and so the English typically had a very negative view of Jews as greedy, dishonest moneylenders who probably wanted to kill Christians. It would be very easy for Violet to smear them.[3]

As with almost all of Violet's schemes, this one was personal. Violet knew a Spanish merchant residing in London—a man he called Anthony Fernando, but whose legal name was Antonio Fernandez Carvajal. Carvajal had lived in London since the 1630s. He was a Spanish national who regularly went to Catholic Mass at the residence of the Spanish ambassador. It was fairly common at this time for foreign merchants to set up a permanent station in London to take advantage of the English market. Carvajal himself imported silver and gold from the West Indies and Cadiz, respectively, but also imported a wide range of goods—hats, brushes, and knives—from all over western Europe. While he had been fined once or twice for not attending Protestant church services in the 1640s, he was allowed to stay in London because of a special dispensation for foreign merchants residing in England legally. Carvajal was a respected merchant in London and, because he traded in gold and silver, it is not surprising that he had business dealings with his neighbor, the goldsmith Thomas Violet. Such a man seemed to be prospering in the world, and he was. Yet Carvajal was living a lie. For Carvajal was not in fact a Catholic, but a Jew.[4]

It had been illegal to be a Jew in Spain since 1492; the Jews who had not fled the country that year had gone underground. Called Marranos, these Jews pretended to be Catholics but kept their true religion in private. Spanish Jews, like Carvajal, often participated in international trade; and, in fact, many lived in England during the sixteenth and seventeenth centuries—even though it was illegal for Jews to reside in England. They hid in plain sight, just as they lived in Spain. More sophisticated merchants were aware that they were Jews, but in an almost "don't ask, don't tell" environment, no one called the Jews out because, at least in England, they often had valuable trading contacts, as Carvajal had. It was better to do business with them than to out them to the authorities.

However, all of this changed in the mid-1650s. A variety of historical trends converged to force the Jews in London to publicly announce themselves at that time. Intellectual changes in European society in the previous century and a half had started transforming Christian Europeans' understanding of Jews. First and foremost, the Reformation caused a growing interest among the English in both the Old Testament and Hebrew. By exposing themselves to Hebrew throughout the sixteenth and seventeenth centuries, English scholars came to have a great interest in and appreciation of contemporary Jewish writings.[5] Then in the early 1650s, a Dutch Jew named Menasseh ben Israel broached the subject of legally readmitting Jews into England. Menasseh ben Israel, an important rabbi, scholar, and theologian in Amsterdam, had convinced himself that "he was destined to promote the coming of the Messiah."[6] Ben Israel communicated with English theologians throughout the 1640s and, by 1649, had persuaded himself that the new English Republic would be the harbinger of the Messiah. He was drawn to this view after reading several European accounts that claimed the Native Americans of North and South America were, in fact, the ten Lost Tribes of Israel.[7] Because he believed that there were Jews in the New World, ben Israel felt that if the Jews could return to England, they would fulfill the prophecy that the restoration of the Holy Land would only occur after Jews had scattered all over the earth. Since they were already in the Americas, they only had to colonize England to bring about this long-hoped-for event.[8]

Menasseh ben Israel published a pamphlet in England in 1652 laying out these claims. In it, he celebrated the new English Republic and explained that its leaders should know "how acceptable to God you are" by creating their new nation. Indeed, he asserted that "the whole world stands amazed at these things, and the eyes of all are turned upon you, that they may see whither all these things . . . have [been] fore-told by the Prophets."[9] Such flattering praise of the new government actually inspired Parliament to debate whether or not it should allow Jews back into England in 1653.[10] This occurred not only because of ben Israel's pamphlet, but also due to a widespread feeling among Puritan ministers that if Jews were allowed back into England, they could finally be exposed to the true form of Christianity, then convert, and, with any luck, bring the Second Coming of Christ. Hence both Menasseh ben Israel and important Independent divines came to the same conclusion: the Messiah would only return to earth when Jews lived in England. When the Anglo-Dutch War ended in 1654, political obstacles to further discussions were eased, and by September 1655, the readmission of the Jews was the talk of London.

Clearly interested in the topic, Oliver Cromwell's government opened a dialogue with Menasseh ben Israel in November 1655. Despite some public opposition, Cromwell was so encouraged by these talks that in December of that year, he called a conference at Whitehall where Jewish readmission was the sole topic of conversation. He hoped that by inviting concerned parties— particularly leading ministers and merchants in London—he could create a clear and aboveboard framework for Jewish readmission. By bringing both supporters and opponents of readmission into a single gathering, Cromwell imagined that rational discourse and argument would bring all around to his view.[11] Many ministers spoke in favor of readmission, but many merchants opposed it, fearing that Dutch Jews would colonize England and that their trading connections with religious confederates in Holland would undercut English commerce. Since the first Anglo-Dutch War had ended only a year before, these critiques had merit.[12] There was also, of course, fear that allowing the Jews to enter the country was "to blaspheme Christ."[13]

Despite the disputes at the Whitehall Conference about readmitting the Jews, there was a good chance that the conference would have recommended allowing the Jews legally back into the country. However, the whole project stalled when ben Israel, having discovered Jews already living in the country, forced them to proclaim themselves. When they did so, they split the ministers at the conference who favored readmission. Some ministers were delighted that there were already Jews in England ready to be converted to Christianity. Others, however, who had been willing to discuss the topic when it was theoretical, pulled their support for readmission when faced with the reality of Jews already living in London. With the merchants and some ministers against it, the readmission project failed.[14]

Nonetheless, the Whitehall Conference had made the Jews of London public figures and known to Cromwell. Further, during the conference, relations with Spain were deteriorating (leading in fact toward war). Since the Jews living in England were Spanish subjects, they risked losing their property in Spanish territory. In a famous case, a Jewish merchant named Antonio Rodrigues Robles asked Cromwell to help protect his property in Spanish territory in November 1655. Cromwell agreed. With this in mind, and with their public exposure and the failure of the Whitehall Conference, it is clear why Robles, Menasseh ben Israel, Carvajal, and other Jews of London had to petition Cromwell on March 24, 1656, to allow them legal residency status. While the petition was never officially acted upon, Cromwell's government energetically protected Anglo-Jewish property overseas and this let the Jews of London know that they were now de facto legal residents of England. [15]

All of this mattered to Violet because an anti-Jewish reaction quickly appeared in England. Presbyterian ministers wrote pamphlets against the Jews highlighting the threat they posed to the religious purity of the land. English merchants complained that the Jews would hurt their own businesses. While Violet was sympathetic to the merchants' worries, he faced a more personal assault by the Jews. Violet's neighbor, Antonio Fernandez Carvajal, set up the first synagogue in London just blocks away from Violet's house. Carvajal's new synagogue on Creechurch Lane was just down the street from Violet's home. The synagogue was a large building that could hold more than a hundred-person congregation. Carvajal even brought his cousin, Rabbi Moses Athias, to lead the congregation. By 1657, the synagogue was up and running and clearly there to stay; Carvajal signed a twenty-one-year lease on the building. [16] The Jews went to synagogue twice a day—at around 7 a.m. and then again at 3 p.m. Londoners gawked at the sight and often went and watched the ceremonies. At the time, Jewish services were conducted by the cantor and were comprised almost entirely of singing in Hebrew. The Christian English enjoyed mocking the Jews' songs. Violet did not see the humor in the situation, but instead was extremely irritated that people would attend this neighborhood synagogue twice a day and create a terrible racket. Violet's anger, combined with his envy of Carvajal's success, inspired him to include the Jews in his plot against Pight. [17]

Violet laid the groundwork for his scheme by building relationships with his new neighbors. He began dropping by the synagogue and made himself known to Rabbi Moses Athias. Discovering that the rabbi was from Hamburg, Violet suggested he help the congregation strike a commemorative coin for the Jews to celebrate the accession of the new Holy Roman Emperor, Leopold I, in 1658 (Hamburg was in the Holy Roman Empire). After establishing himself as someone the Jews could do business with, Violet began to implement his scheme to use the Jews to help him acquire Richard Pight's post at the Royal Mint.

To put his plan into motion Violet needed a dupe. He chose a pewterer named Tobias Knowles. Violet took Knowles to the synagogue to meet with Rabbi Athias, or as Violet called him, Rabbi Moses. There, Violet explained to the rabbi that Knowles knew coins and could help them acquire foreign coins to purchase goods in the Holy Roman Empire. Violet took Knowles to Fish Street and told him in private that he wanted Knowles to bring the Jews patterns of foreign coins and ask them which they wanted. When they picked one, Knowles should take the sample to Richard Pight, whose job was to prevent the illegal production of foreign coins, and tell him the Jews wanted a large order of them. Knowles was to offer Pight a bribe to look the other way and not persecute the Jews.[18]

Violet stressed to Knowles that he should not tell Pight that Violet was responsible for the Jews' request. Knowles told Violet that he feared that the whole thing was illegal because, while making foreign coins was not as serious a crime as counterfeiting English coins, it was still against the law and he could still pay a terrible price if caught doing so. Violet assured him not to worry. Even if their actions were illegal, Violet had friends on the Council of State and in Parliament who would give them an "Act of Indemnity" that would forgive any possible illegal action. Yet, he added, they were not going to do anything illegal, so Knowles had nothing to worry about. Convinced by Violet that he was in no danger, Knowles followed his advice.[19]

Knowles went to Pight and asked if he could mint counterfeit foreign coins for the Jews. Pight told Knowles (by Knowles's account) that it was legal for him to do so as long as he did not counterfeit any English coins. Knowles then "cast about 400 Pieces . . . of Copper and Brass." Knowles now imagined he was involved in an honest business deal. He delivered the coins to Violet and told him he was ready to sell them to the Jews. Then, Violet revealed his plan. The whole point of the transaction was to entrap both the Jews and Pight in the act of illegally producing and selling foreign coins. Violet informed Knowles that his friends in both Parliament and the Council of State would support Violet's scheme if he proved that the Jews were illegally buying foreign coins and that Pight was allowing them to do so. All of them would be arrested and their property forfeited. Pight's job would come to Violet as well as half of the Jews' assets. The Jews, after having to pay their fines, would flee the country. Stunned by Violet's revelations, Knowles objected that if he was caught with the Jews in some illegal act, he too might be prosecuted. Violet assured him that his connections would protect Knowles and that he would actually share in the reward.[20]

Violet told Knowles that his efforts could really make the plan work—if he followed Violet's instructions. Knowles had to arrange to meet the Jews in a tavern. It was critical that he bring the four hundred struck coins with him. When the Jews arrived, Violet's connections in the Tower of London would help him arrest the Jews in the act of buying the illegal coins, destroying them and Pight in one swift stroke. Knowles pointed out that no one would know he was Violet's accomplice in this action except Violet, a fact that led him to fret that he might be charged with illegally producing foreign coins. Violet told him not to worry. Knowles clearly did, though, and continued to press the issue. Violet got angry and finally told Knowles that if he did not follow through with his part of the plan "Violet would stab . . . [Knowles] the next time he met him."[21]

Knowles was frightened and did not know what to do. He went home and decided that he should back out of the whole affair. Thomas Violet was clearly not a man to be trusted, and Knowles worried he would get involved in a dispute between Violet and Pight that would only go poorly for him. So Knowles melted the coins meant for the Jews and did not do what Violet asked. But at that point, Knowles really fell into a trap. Pight had actually allowed him to produce the illegal foreign coins to snare Knowles and arrest him for his actions. Pight, thus, was much like Violet. On February 24, 1659, Knowles was brought before the Old Bailey (a London court) on those charges. Knowles testified about what happened and the whole world suddenly knew that both Pight and Violet would do anything to anyone in an effort to advance their own agendas.[22]

What happened next is not entirely clear. It is very likely that Violet and Pight saw each other in the streets of London and Violet attacked Pight—not once, but twice, in front of witnesses. Meanwhile, Violet started petitioning the Council of State around January 1660 that Pight and Knowles were working together to illegally produce foreign currency in England.[23] Pight responded by commissioning a pamphlet detailing how Thomas Violet was about the worst person in the world. Thomas Violet was a man who feared

neither God nor man, nor to destroy the life of any man though it were his own
Father, so he could but obtain his own wicked ends; This being the opinion of
all that know him, and is generally said of him, having as bad a name as ever I
heard man have; Pray take this ensuing discovery taken before some of the
Justices of the Peace; which he so boldly cites in divers his printed papers by
the oaths of honest men . . . and whether it be the common good or his own
private lucre he intends to promote by it, let any rational man judge. [24]

Pight's assessment of Violet is accurate; Thomas Violet worked for no one
beyond himself.

Neither Pight nor Violet could gain government backing, however, since
they were fighting during one of the most tumultuous six-month periods in
English history. By the end of 1659, England had had four governments in
one year. It was not clear who ruled the country, and, in fact, no one seemed
to have any clear authority at all. The most powerful force on the British Isles
was the army that occupied Scotland, led by General George Monck, who
controlled his army because he could still pay it. Monck had uneasily
watched the political collapse in 1659, and on January 1, 1660, he decided to
take control and marched his army south. By February he was in London.
The government then sitting was the Rump Parliament—the Parliament that
had executed Charles I and run the English Republic from 1649 to 1653. [25] At
first, the Rump Parliament thought that Monck was on its side, but on February 11, he made it clear that he was not. Monck informed the Members of
Parliament that they would order a free election for a Parliament whose
purpose would be to put an end to the current uncertainty. In a free election,
the Royalists and Presbyterians would win—and vote to bring back the monarchy. Charles I's son, Charles II, had lived in exile for more than a decade,
but the young man was eager to become England's king. Once Monck announced to the people of London what he had done, there was a great shout
and then spontaneous parties in the streets. The people of London were tired
of war, high taxes, and political uncertainty. They were willing to try a king
again. [26]

Charles II helped out his cause by pledging that he would not punish
anyone for their role in the Civil Wars—except the regicides. Charles arrived
from exile on May 29, 1660, to enthusiastic and happy crowds. As a reward
to Monck, Charles made him the Duke of Albemarle. Together, the king and
the general rode into London to the cheers of an adoring people. It was not
that people were suddenly ready to give up their political rights, but rather
that the experiment in republican government clearly failed because the lead-

ers of the government could not find a way to control the three kingdoms without using armies of occupation. The English were tired of paying the very high taxes necessary to maintain those armies, and looked forward to peace, low taxes, and prosperity.

Violet seized the opportunity that the Restoration of the monarchy provided. He petitioned Charles II for a position as "Registrar and Searcher of Gold and Silver" to be exported by the East India Company. He also asked to be an officer of the Royal Mint overseeing gold and silver production. This would be restitution for the £20,000 that he claimed he lost in the service of the king over the previous twenty years. Charles thanked him for his petition and said he would look into Violet's request. Violet may have been over-reaching a bit—claiming that instead of losing about £8,000 or £11,000, he was now owed £20,000. Yet in the heady first months of the Restoration, Violet and many other Royalists who lost property and positions during the preceding twenty years had high hopes for compensation. Charles II wanted to give it to them and he may have even promised Violet a manor in payment for his efforts for the Royalist cause during the wars.[27]

Unfortunately for Charles II, the Royalists, and Thomas Violet, it quickly became clear that for Charles to keep the peace, he would not be able to return any of the land that people lost during the Civil Wars. To do so would be to throw out the current possessors and deeply anger many Presbyterians. Former Royalists like Violet would not be getting any compensation for land or money lost for the Royalist cause. Further, Violet's was not a unique case. In fact, "so many [Royalist] gentry crowded into London to hunt" for employment "that prices there soared. . . . It was a gold rush atmosphere, with disappointment inevitable for most."[28] All of this may have become clear to Violet in the fall of 1660, because he decided to attack the Jews again.

The Jews were in a precarious position in the fall of 1660. They had never been legally admitted into the country by Cromwell, and now Charles II was under no legal or moral obligation to allow them to stay. Further, in London, the Jews had many religious and economic enemies who would have been happy to see them leave—after they took the Jews' property. Violet knew this and decided to persuade Charles II that the Jews were a dangerous threat to English religious and economic life. Violet had thought as early as December 1659 that he could bring a case against the Jews in English court arguing that they were not living in the country legally and consequently should either be forced to leave or pay an enormous fine. Violet brought his idea to judge Thomas Tyrell, who informed Violet that because of the uncertain political situation, he should wait until things settled down before he moved forward with the plan. Tyrell even hinted that the best time to do this would be when the monarchy was restored. So Violet waited, and as soon as the king came back, he returned to Tyrell in June 1660 ready to move against the Jews. Tyrell told Violet to produce a petition against the Jews, which he would present to the king's Privy Council.[29]

Violet put his plans against the Jews on hold while he was petitioning for a position to oversee the East India Company's gold.[30] While he did so, a group of English merchants presented a petition to the king on November 30, 1660, demanding that the Jews be expelled. Probably presented by Sir William Courtney, it explained why the Jews were so dangerous to the English. During the Middle Ages, the petition claimed, the Jews had used their money to purchase special privileges. This led them to be able to practice "ill-dealings" and "oppressions" of decent English folk. After they were rightly banished by Edward I in 1290 "at the desire of the whole kingdom," everyone was much better off. Then, the Jews returned in the mid-1650s. In the few years that the Jews had been in London, they had allegedly "renewed their usurious and fraudulent practices." They had "flourish[ed] so much that they endeavored to buy St. Paul's for a synagogue." Since St. Paul's Cathedral is the largest and most important Christian structure in London, this was a very serious allegation. In order to stop such horrible activities, the merchants asked the king and Parliament to impose "heavy Taxes" on the Jews, then seize "their personal property" and finally impose "banishment for residence without [a] license."[31]

The London Jews knew that they had to respond to this attack. Seven days later they sent Antonio Carvajal's widow, Maria, to petition Parliament. Carvajal "had died on 2 November 1659 after an unsuccessful operation to remove what was most likely a kidney or bladder stone." Carvajal was, in some ways, the anti-Violet. Unlike Thomas, he was well liked by people who knew him. When he died in 1659 he "was honored by a special knell of the bells of St Katharine Creechurch."[32] Since Carvajal was wealthy and well connected, his widow, Maria, would have been able to take advantage of these contacts when she presented a counterpetition to Charles II on December 7. Charles decided to pass both petitions (the pro and con) to Parliament so the members could discuss the issue. On December 18, Parliament took up the matter.[33]

Violet found out about the merchants' petition in December and hurriedly brought his own petition to the king and Parliament on December 18, 1660.

Unfortunately, there is no record of the debate in Parliament about the topic, so it is not clear if the members discussed Violet's petition. However, the text of Violet's note survives and it reveals what he wanted the government to do with the Jews: Violet spells out in great detail why Jews threatened the Christian religion in England. He reminded his readers of passages in the New Testament that portray Jews in a negative light. These verses should inform the English, Violet wrote, that because God had spurned the Jews, the English should do no less. Violet also noted that numerous English laws explicitly prohibited members of different faiths from living in the country. Allowing Jews in the country would be like allowing Catholics to flourish. At the time, anti-Catholicism was one thing virtually all English people could agree on, so when put in that context, it likened the government that supported Jews to one that protected the devil.[34]

Even though he was deceased, the person Violet held up for particular vilification was Antonio Carvajal. Violet had seen Carvajal go to the Spanish ambassador's house to Mass "daily." That this man, who had pretended to be a devout Catholic, should then publicly announce that he was a Jew just began to hint at how conniving these people were. Then, while Violet did not mention Carvajal by name in the next couple of paragraphs, his accusations about what "Jews" did read like a description of Carvajal's business practices. Violet said that Jews were involved in complex import/export schemes and were "adulterers of all manner of Merchandize."[35] They made money on commodities like wine but also in the export or gold and silver. Finally, Violet said that in conversations with Carvajal, he discovered that the wealthy Jewish merchant had promised Oliver Cromwell £1,000,000 in return for allowing two thousand Jewish merchant families to move into England. Their goal would be nothing less than to take over English trade and, very likely, destroy the Christian faith.[36]

Violet's solution to this threat to English life was quite simple. He wanted King Charles II to "take these Jewish men and Women, whom you will find in London, in the net of the Law." He should do this because "God hath put these People into your Majesties hands to help to stop the great debts of the Nation I humbly say." For "Jews are Blasphemers against Christ, and I humbly pray their Purse and Bodies may pay for it."[37] If Charles imprisoned all of the Jews in London, they would be ransomed at great price by their fellow Jews around the world. Violet claimed that all the Jews in the world were related, and rich, and would be more than willing to pay a fortune in ransom money. After all, Antonio Carvajal, "the great Jew," had told Violet that they were willing to bribe Oliver Cromwell with £1,000,000 just to bring people into England. Who knows how much they might pay to ransom their own?[38]

Violet finally appealed to Charles's sense of his place in history. Violet warned the king that if he allowed the Jews to stay, then "when the History of the present times shall be writ," the "after ages" would judge him harshly.[39] Ignoring the Jewish presence would be akin to letting in Catholics, destroying Protestantism, and annihilating English traders. In fact, it would be a calamity. To prevent this condemnation by posterity, Charles needed to banish the Jews, but not before receiving a massive ransom from their foreign relatives to let them go. Also, Thomas Violet needed to receive a percentage of the Jews' fortunes for all his hard work in bringing this important issue to the king.[40]

In this particular case, Violet's petition fell on deaf ears. He may have failed because of timing. Violet presented his petition to Parliament on December 18, but only eleven days later Charles dissolved Parliament. After an election that spring, Parliament did not convene again until May 8, 1661. Without a sitting Parliament, and with no record of the report of the debate on December 18, it is not clear what Charles and the leaders in Parliament wanted to do with this issue. It may simply have been lost in the dissolving of one Parliament and the calling of another. But there might have been something else to this. It might have been Charles himself.[41]

Charles initially hoped to have a much more tolerant religious policy than his father. In fact, Charles wanted "to become accepted as an arbiter and protector" of all religious factions in England—including Catholics. Charles would eventually have to retreat from this position over the course of 1661, yet he would not have thought to do so in December 1660 and January 1661. That winter Charles noted that while there was little public support for Jews in England, neither were there good reasons to expel them. In fact, their business connections might make the English Crown money. Further, Charles's religious tolerance likely included Jews. If that is true, then Violet's charge about the verdict of history was reversed. Charles ignored Violet's advice about the Jews and he was not condemned as an anti-Semite. This label, though, fits very well on Thomas Violet.[42]

NOTES

1. Challis, "Lord Hastings to the Great Silver Recoinage, 1464–1699," 329; See also Thomas Violet, *The Answer of the Corporation of Moniers in the Mint* (London, 1653); Thomas Violet, *Proposal Humbly Presented to His Highness Oliver* (London, 1656); Thomas Violet, *To his Highness* (London, 1656).

2. Hessayon, "'The Great Trappaner of England,'" 211.

3. Anthony Julius, *Trials of the Diaspora: A History of Anti-Semitism in England* (Oxford: Oxford University Press, 2010), 242–46.

4. Gardiner, *History of the Commonwealth and Protectorate*, vol. 3, 218; Katz, *The Jews in the History of England 1485–1850*, 134; Hessayon, "'The Great Trappaner of England,'" 217–18; Violet, *A True Narrative of som remarkable-Procedings*, 38.

5. David Katz, *Philo-Semitism and the Readmission of the Jews to England 1603–1655* (Oxford: Oxford University Press, 1982), passim.

6. Lucien Wolf, editor's introduction to *Menasseh ben Israel's Mission to Oliver Cromwell: Being a Reprint of the Pamphlets Published by Menasseh ben Israel to Promote the Re-Admission of the Jews to England, 1649–1656*, by Menasseh ben Israel, ed. Lucien Wolf (London: Macmillan, 1901), xxiii.

7. Ibid., xxiv.

8. Ibid., xxii–xxvi.

9. Menasseh ben Israel, *The Hope of Israel* (London, 1652), 4, 5.

10. John Thurloe, *A Collection of State Papers of John Thurloe*, vol. 1 (London: n.p., 1742), 387.

11. The best description of this process is found in Katz, *Philo-Semitism and the Readmission of the Jews to England*, 190–231. See also *CSPD, 1655*, 336, and *CSPD, 1655–56*, 15–16.

12. [H. Jessey, attrib. author], *A narrative of the Late Proceeds at White-Hall* (London, 1656), 3–8.

13. *CSPD, 1655–56*, 51.

14. John Dury, *A Case of Conscience, Whether it be lawful to Admit Jews into a Christian Commonwealth?* (London, 1656), 1–9.

15. Katz, *The Jews in the History of England*, 107–34; *CSPD, 1655–56*, 237.

16. Hessayon, "'The Great Trappaner of England,'" 210–11, 218–19.

17. Thomas Violet, *A Petition against the Jews* (London, 1661), 1–2; Pepys, 313.

18. Anon., *The Great Trappanner of England Discovered*, 2–3.

19. Ibid., 3–4.

20. Ibid., 3.

21. Ibid., 4.

22. Ibid., 2.

23. Thomas Violet, *To the Supreme Authority the Parliament of England* (London, 1660), 3, passim; *CSPD, 1660*, 448.

24. Anon., *The Great Trappanner of England Discovered*, 2.

25. In the very confusing politics of the period, the Rump Parliament, which ruled England as a Republic for nearly five years, was brought back to run the country twice by the army in 1659–60. In both cases it lacked almost all authority and failed to operate as an effective government.

26. Woolrych, *Britain in Revolution*, 762–63, Pepys, *The Diary of Samuel Pepys*, 15–16.

27. *CSPD, 1660*, 249; *CSPD, 1660–61*, 271–72.

28. Ronald Hutton, *The Restoration* (Oxford: Oxford University Press, 1986), 137.

29. Violet, *A Petition against the Jews*, 7–8.

30. *CSPD, 1660–61*, p. 271; Violet, *A Petition against the Jews*, section 2, 10 (sig. Bbv).

31. *CSPD, 1660–61*, 366.

32. Hessayon, "'The Great Trappaner of England,'" 224.

33. Katz, *The Jews in the History of England*, 140–41; *CJ*, vol. 8, 209.

34. Violet, *A Petition against the Jews*, 3–5.

35. Ibid., 4.

36. Ibid., 4–5, 7.

37. Ibid., 6.

38. Ibid., 7.

39. Ibid., 5.

40. Violet, *A Petition against the Jews*, 5, 7–8. See Anon., *The Great Trappanner of England Discovered*, for evidence of Violet's desire for a cut in the profits.

41. *CJ*, vol. 8, 244–45.

42. Hutton, *The Restoration*, 166.

Chapter Eight

Roman

During the Restoration, Violet tried other ways to find a permanent source of income besides swindling the Jews and framing Richard Pight. In the months from June 1660 through January 1662, Violet presented four different types of petitions to Charles II's new government. As with most of his ideas over the previous thirty years, the petitions were designed to do three things: expand English trade, increase the English government's revenue, and improve Thomas Violet's finances. Violet pursued the same strategy that brought him success in the 1630s: convince the monarch to give him regulatory power over how some segment of the English economy used its money.

Violet's scheme for getting the king's overburdened government to listen to him was threefold. First, he emphasized his loyalty to Charles I during the Civil Wars and the financial and personal hardship he endured during the 1640s and 1650s. Then, Violet claimed that all of his actions during the 1650s were designed not to help, but to hurt the English Republic and Cromwell's Protectorate. Finally, he explained how his expertise in coin production and trade gave him a special set of skills that would make him invaluable to the king because any one of his plans would ensure a huge new stream of revenue for the cash-strapped government.

In a series of petitions to the king, Violet spelled out in great detail the sufferings he endured for the Royalist cause during the Civil Wars. He explained that "for my Loyalty I have been most Barbarously used." Violet then rewrote his own history during the struggle, blending fact and exaggeration in a heady brew of self-justification. According to Violet, in 1643 Parliament asked him to "discover the transporters of Gold and Silver, and . . . raise the Parliament monies by the fines of the offenders." Further, "I was to raise the Parliament forty Thousand pounds by the fines of the transporters of Gold." Violet claimed to have struck this deal with Parliament on November 10, 1643. As soon as he had done so, though, then along "Comes your Majesties Fathers Letter . . . and commands me not to do this service for the Parliament at my peril." Violet bravely decided not to be Parliament's agent in fining merchants who exported gold and silver out of the country, but rather he "chose Poverty and Loyalty before Riches."[1]

In order to obey the king, Violet claimed that he made an excuse to Parliament for not collecting its money, saying that he could not catch the "French and Dutch Merchants . . . that had transported the gold and silver out of the Nation" because they "were removed from Dover" and out of his reach. At that point, two members of Parliament named "Whitaker and Corbet" moved against Violet "and said I was your Majesties Royal Fathers Spie, a Cavalier and Malignant, and moved the House against me." Then, "They sent me to the King's bench; and there I remained a Prisoner."[2] This of course is not what happened. Violet did speak to Parliament about transporting gold, but on March 18, 1641—before the king and Parliament irrevocably split.[3] He first came into Parliament's custody not because of the spying charge, but because he had not paid £70 in taxes. He was arrested on June 20, 1643, for this delinquency, sent to Peter's House jail, and sometime later in the year transferred to the King's Bench.[4] When in prison, he became a Royalist, and in December 1643 was part of a prisoner exchange for Arthur Haselrig, an important member of the Roundhead faction. Violet made his own sacrifice sound that much more impressive because instead of being imprisoned for not paying £70 in taxes, he now said he had been incarcerated because he chose not to collect £40,000 in fines for Parliament.[5]

After the prisoner exchange, which occurred around Christmas Day 1643, Violet went up to Oxford where Charles I asked him to take the infamous letter back to London asking the London merchants to support the king rather than Parliament. One of the central themes of all of Violet's writings during this period (1660–62) was his unjust arrest for bringing the king's letter to the merchants and Parliament's illegal seizure of his property. At various times, he blamed John Wollaston or famous Members of Parliament such as Henry Vane, Arthur Haselrig, and Oliver St. John for illegally arresting him. One thing that changed from his earlier writings to his 1660–62 descriptions of his imprisonment was his account of how long he had been incarcerated. During the 1640s and 1650s, he claimed he spent nearly four years in the

Tower of London, of which 928 days were under close guard. But in 1662, he said he spent eight years all told in prison if he counted the time in King's Bench jail before the Tower of London and King's Bench jail after he was released from the Tower. It is true that he was transferred from the Tower to King's Bench on October 1, 1647, so he was certainly imprisoned for some time after that. However, by July 1649, he was in Essex trying to get his estate back and in 1650 he was spending all day at the Council of State. So it is not clear how he arrived at "about eight years" in prison for the king—especially when he never said that he was incarcerated that long before the Restoration.[6]

After saying that he suffered eight years' imprisonment for the king's father, Violet explained to Charles II how much money he had lost during his time in the Tower of London. He noted that he had to pay £700 to maintain himself over that period. At the time his entire estate was sequestered by Parliament, Violet estimated that his estate was worth £11,000. However, when he added up all the lost revenue he should have earned from his position as overseer of the gold and silver wire drawers, as well as his estates' incomes, he decided that he had lost £20,000 in the king's service. Violet told Charles II that the loss of his estate led to "his total ruin." Further, he "could never obtain any part of his estate . . . without" Charles giving it back to him.[7]

Violet felt he had proven how loyal he was to the king's cause in the 1640s and how much it hurt him financially. He then went on to show how all of his well-documented support for the Commonwealth in the 1650s was actually an effort to help the Royalists. Violet was not the only former Royalist who had to publicly repudiate his actions under the Commonwealth, but Violet found himself in a particularly difficult situation. He needed to prove that all of the pamphlets he wrote in the 1650s declaring his support for the Republic and the Protectorate from 1650 to 1659 in fact were lies and that his efforts to strengthen the Republic's economy by helping it claim £276,000 of silver were somehow a ploy to weaken the Commonwealth. It was a large task, but Violet was up to it.

Violet told Charles II that if Charles asked his father's "old Trusty Servants" Thomas Davis, Humphrey Painter, and David Ramadg (respectively, Charles I's barber, surgeon, and servant), he would find that these men knew Violet well and spoke to him in November 1652 about the silver ships. Violet said that "we four made a solemn promise of secrecy one to another for the concealing of what I then imparted to them in November 1652 and several

times since." Violet spoke to them because he knew that they were all loyal
Royalists and he wanted the king to hear that

> I told them I would stay the Dutch silver in the ships *Samson, Salvador*, and
> *Saint George*, and I did at the same time show them a parchment Roll which
> was several reasons to engage the Parliament and the Dutch in a war, that I
> would stay the silver in these ships at my own great expense, which I did upon
> the grounds that it would destroy the present Parliament and Council of State. [8]

Violet told Davis, Painter, and Ramadg that "I would sell myself to my
shirt . . . [to] stay the said silver in the ships." He wanted to start "a war both
with Holland, Spain, [and] Hamborough [*sic*]." Violet went on to say that in
November 1652, Parliament was losing the Anglo-Dutch War, and if it had
had to fight a war on two other fronts, he hoped that it would be weakened
enough that the Royal party could come back from exile and take the country
away "from the Parliament, Cromwell, or any other fanatic Rebel." [9]

In case the testimony of servants was not enough to prove his loyalty,
Violet also said that his "close kinsmen" Lieutenant Colonel Paul Smith
could also support his testimony. Violet claimed that on December 13, 1652,
he and Smith went together by boat to visit the three silver ships and Violet
told Smith that he was doing everything in his power to "divide and destroy
both . . . Parliament and the Council of State." Violet also virtuously noted
that Smith had long been under surveillance by Bradshaw and Cromwell and
that "often I have saved his life within this twelve years, when several warrants for high treason as a spy . . . was for the apprehending him." But Violet
"hid and concealed" Smith and "got him passed by a wrong name several
times, both at Gravesend and Dover." [10] In this case, Violet was connecting
himself to a well-known and respected Royalist. Paul Smith was in fact a
Royalist agent who worked tirelessly in the 1650s for the Royalist cause and
he was known to Charles II. When Violet touted that he "furnished Col.
Smith with several sums of money to make his escape, which since he hath
justly paid me," Violet was highlighting his Royalist credentials. [11]

While the above evidence was plausible, it did not prove that Violet was
an active Royalist during the 1650s. Rather, it showed he could grumble with
fellow ex-Royalists and help out a cousin in need. But Violet was only using
these examples to lay the groundwork for his biggest claim yet—that he was
the person responsible for Cromwell's military coup on April 20, 1653. Violet declared that he decided in November 1652 that he would prevent Parliament from acquiring the bullion from the silver ships. He managed to do so

for nearly six months, during which time Oliver Cromwell became very angry with Parliament. Finally, on April 16, Violet convinced Cromwell "to seize the silver [and] dissolve the Parliament." Cromwell listened to Violet and on April 20, 1653, he dissolved Parliament and a few days later took the silver. Thus Violet could brag, "I did . . . with a Goose Quill, that ten thousand Muskets could not have done by force; it was a desperate undertaking, and had not God enable[d] me . . . I [would have] sunk in the undertaking [of] this business." Violet asserted that the only person who suspected he was preventing the silver from getting out was "Sir Henry Vane" (a member of the Council of State) who "had the best Nose of all . . . for he smelt me out, and would have had me committed to the Tower for staying this silver, but God delivered me from him." Violet concluded his petition to Charles II with the aside that he could have taken a £10,000 bribe to allow the silver to leave the country, but he instead "chose to live on bread and water, and to borrow fifteen hundred pounds to enable me to stay this silver" and destroy the king's great enemy—Parliament.[12]

Of course, Violet's story contradicted all of his public acts during the Interregnum. But there was no one who could come forward to deny Violet's accusations because the leading players were either dead, about to be executed as regicides, or could only confirm that Violet was part of the effort to capture the Dutch silver. This was a good thing, too, because he had actually spent the whole winter of 1652–53 in the Council of State trying to get his share of the silver.

When bragging about how he destroyed Parliament, Violet gives himself away, in an almost Freudian slip, when he writes he hated the "many men [who,] when they have made use of a man for their own ends, forget their promises."[13] He could not help but reveal his anger at the Rump Parliament for not paying him his £11,000. Yet because Violet failed in that effort to acquire his money, he could claim the whole enterprise was a fraud designed to bring down Parliament. So instead of a traitor of the worst kind, Violet portrayed himself as one of the great Royalist heroes of the 1650s. Further, his cousin Paul Smith, a legitimate Royalist secret agent in the 1650s, corroborated what Violet said. Smith testified that Violet "hath several times assisted me, to make me my escape, when there was warrants upon a charge of High Treason . . . for my apprehending, and hath gotten me passed beyond Seas by a wrong name."[14]

Unfortunately for Violet, Smith's report proved only that he and Violet had a conversation and that Violet helped a relative in trouble. It was enough, however, for Violet to feel that he had proved to the king that he was a war hero of the highest order and that he deserved a reward. Such a prize was well earned because Violet had lost so much for the king. But he did not just ask for recompense for his losses. Violet also offered to make the king money while earning income for himself. Violet's first, and potentially most lucrative, idea was to regulate the East India Company. He would have also liked to have controlled the Levant Company, but he focused his energies on the East India Company. The problem with the East India Company was that it had to use English gold and silver to buy Indian goods. Violet claimed that "the English Gold and Silver hath bin melted down, and sold by Goldsmiths to the East-India Company and Goldsmiths have gotten Merchants to sell English Gold and Silver in Ingots, to send to the East Indies."[15] Unlike the Dutch, who conquered and settled cities in Asia where they manufactured items for the locals to buy, the English went with "our hats in our hands, and shuffle from Port to Port at the courtesy of the Natives in the East-Indies." If the East India Company copied the Dutch and moved into Asian cities, it needed to have its gold and silver supply regulated to better guarantee its success. Violet asked that the "East India Company be forced to register all gold and silver" it sent overseas and that, as Violet wrote, "I humbly desire . . . to be register for the King." Despite his plea that his plan would help the company, no one responded to Violet's request.[16]

Undaunted, Violet then told the government he could help with the regulation of gold and silver exports more generally. Violet told the king's men, "I heard . . . that the Merchants declared they would Transport Gold and Silver, if there was profit in it, in spite of all Laws." Further, "there was some Merchants at the Council of Trade, did openly affirm, that Transporting Gold and Silver, if it did produce profit, could not be stopped." Violet informed the king that "if your Lordship command, and empower me to see the Laws already made put in execution, I will force the Merchants . . . to bring in the Gold and Silver every day into the Mint, after it is imported to be coined, or at his peril let him transport it."[17] And he meant it. Violet wrote that "rogues [are] hanged for murders, for robbery, for housebreaking . . . so I say . . . death for any man to transport Gold."[18] On June 19, 1661, Violet asked for an allowance from the King's Mint to help pay him as he searched for merchants illegally transporting gold and silver out of the country.[19] On October 31, he made these proposals to the Customs Board. Intrigued, the board, in turn, on December 18 of that year, asked for the attorney general's opinion on the legality of Violet's proposals.[20]

Once he realized that he finally had the government's attention, Violet tried to influence the Customs Board's decision by revealing another idea he believed would benefit the regime. In this January 25, 1662, petition, he explained to Charles II's government that from 1626 to 1639 the collection of customs duties went especially well under Charles I. Violet said he would like to bring back those halcyon days by setting into motion his "Model plan for collecting customs and preventing abuses." If the king followed his plan, then he would "raise the revenue £100,000 a year above that of 1660." Violet was hoping that by not targeting any individual or corporation, he would not face resistance to his ideas—and that the lure of such a large income might draw the government's interest. Yet his proposals ultimately went nowhere because no one wanted Violet overseeing anything.[21]

As the spring of 1662 wore on, Violet started to despair. It did not appear that Charles II's government would ever find a position for him and, because of that, he would never earn enough money to pay back his creditors. At this point Violet had been living off loans for about fifteen years and his creditors no longer believed that he would settle his debts.

This was not his only financial problem; Violet could not get the people who owed him money to pay him anything. Even the men who held the £2,000 in bonds he had recovered under Oliver Cromwell would not pay him. While this galled Violet, he was also furious about his inability to take control of the lands of William Lenthall. Lenthall owned an estate called Haseley Manor, which Violet thought he would receive from the king in the summer of 1660 as recompense for his losses during the wars. It does appear that Charles II recommended that Violet receive "a lease of Haseley Manor," Oxfordshire, early in the summer of 1660, but in August of that year William Lenthall successfully petitioned Charles II to stop the transfer. William Lenthall was the grandnephew of a famous Member of Parliament also named William Lenthall. The great-uncle was pardoned by Charles II for his acts against the Royalists in the Civil Wars. It may be that someone in Charles's government thought that he could punish the Lenthall family by giving their land away, but then when the king made clear that he wanted to pardon the family, the counterpetition prevented Violet from taking over the property. Whatever the case, for the rest his life and to no avail, Violet demanded that he receive the property—or its value in cash.[22]

Since he could never make any money in his usual way—legally stealing someone's property or position—it begs the question why Violet did not begin working as a goldsmith again. But Violet never gives any indication that he ever thought about that possibility. Perhaps that avenue was not available because everyone hated him. The gold and silver wire drawers did not want to do business with a man who had fined all of them in the late 1630s and early 1640s. The Royalist goldsmiths would not want to employ a man who had worked for the Commonwealth. The goldsmiths who supported Parliament did not want to do business with a man who now publicly claimed to have been betraying them for a decade. And finally, virtually everyone would agree with what a Mr. Strickland told one of Violet's good friends, Captain Swan, about what people thought of Thomas Violet: Violet "was a sly and dangerous fellow" who "is always presenting Propositions unto us which may bear double interpretations." Violet was dishonest, had a vile temper, and graspingly tried to get his hands on whatever money he thought he could claim. Few people liked him, and so no one in Charles II's government was willing to try to help him, particularly when so many other Royalists who lost so much during the Civil Wars were seeking positions from the new government. Violet's reputation helps explain what happened to the lands of William Lenthall. Violet thought they were his, but because he had no real friends in the new government, Violet did not have enough political support to be awarded a large estate—or anything at all. [23]

Violet could have taken responsibility for his actions, apologized to others, and tried to be an honest goldsmith. But that was not for him. Violet did not believe that he had ever done anything wrong, and that, in fact, he was the one betrayed by everyone. His bitterness and rage started slipping into all of his writings. While never a very clear writer and always apt to repeat himself, in his final publications in 1661–62, Violet would write the same paragraph over and over again throughout a fifty- or sixty-page pamphlet, which read like a bitter old man's rant about whatever irked him at the moment—politics, the disrespectful nature of youth, or injustices done to him. Of course, Violet was now, in fact, an old man. Being over fifty years old made him quite elderly in early modern England, where average life expectancy was in the midthirties. He had spent the previous twenty years of his life in a precarious situation, where the money that he once enjoyed was out of his reach. He had never, despite his best efforts, managed to recover it. Further, he did not understand how to get it back. Since Violet clearly felt no remorse for lying to people and hurting them, it probably never occurred to him that being honest and treating people fairly might help him. Besides this rather catastrophic personal failing, Violet also did not understand how his actions were viewed by others. All he knew was that if he had overwhelming evidence that someone was doing something illegal, and if he could prove that to the right people—be they King Charles I, Parliament, Oliver Cromwell, or King Charles II—he could win his fortune. Yet he did not acknowledge that this approach made him a hated man.

For instance, Violet tried to get "above a hundred Merchants and Goldsmiths" excluded from Charles II's general pardon of 1660 because he had proof that they illegally exported gold and silver out of the country. These accusations enraged the goldsmiths and merchants of London. They were taken aback, not just because of the charges, but also because Violet thought to invoke the general pardon. As a way to reconcile the country, Charles II had announced the general pardon before he accepted the throne. It pardoned everyone for their actions during the civil war era except for only the most virulent Republicans of the 1640s and 1650s and the men who actually killed his father. Virtually all Englishmen at this point saw the few excluded as traitors. All told, a few dozen men were exempted from the pardon. Hence, Violet's proposal to place the most important London merchants and goldsmiths on a list with traitors in order to fine them £100,000 was quite shocking. It is not surprising that the government, trying to build public support, ignored Violet's petition.

The petition, though, reveals much about Violet and his interaction with his fellow businessmen in London. By attempting to put the goldsmiths and merchants on this list, Violet publicly announced that they should be viewed on par with the worst traitors in English history. Violet could not see that targeting people this way would make them avoid him, not send business contacts his way, and, in fact, loathe him with a passion. He simply did not understand that slandering people was not the way to make the political and personal connections necessary to enjoy long-term success. Violet may never have learned this lesson because of the tumultuous times he lived through. During the war years and under the Commonwealth and Protectorate, the almost constant crisis mode of all governments meant that their leaders were willing to use men like Violet if they thought those men could help them. As life settled down in the Restoration, Violet's strategy created more enemies than it generated silver for the regime, and the government ignored him. [24]

So it was in part due to his numerous enemies that Violet's quest to find a post under Charles II failed. By the late winter and early spring of 1662 Violet became so afraid that he would never get a new position from King Charles that he believed he would go bankrupt and have to enter debtors' prison. In early modern England, bankrupts were arrested and thrown into prison, at their own expense, until they paid back their creditors. Since a man could not earn any money when he was bankrupt and in jail, it was almost impossible to get out of debtors' prison. In fact, being sent there was little better than a death sentence. Violet started to worry during the months of February and March 1662 that he would end up there because he owed money to at least seventeen people, and he had told them for years that he would pay them back, but he now saw no way to do so. While some of these men were his personal acquaintances, all of them at some point demanded that Violet make good on the hundreds of pounds he owed them.[25]

Under stress and feeling afraid, Violet made his will on April 5, 1662. He had made a will before, on December 24, 1646, in the Tower of London. In that case, he had written and signed his will. This time, he decided to dictate it. In this brief document, he mentions "Mr. Alexander Holt of London Goldsmith" who had given "many favors" and "Sumes of Money" to Violet. Violet made Holt his beneficiary. Violet singled Holt out because "I have borrowed of him [money] without which I would have utterly perished." With this literal debt on his mind, Violet willed all of his money and estate to Holt. Violet specifically left any relatives out of his will. He said, "as for my kindred I have none that I care for or that of late years have obliged mee to do for them."[26] In these brief sentences, Violet reveals his values: he only cared about the person to whom he owed the greatest amount of money and he ignored his relations because they had not "obliged" him in recent years.

A few days after Violet made his will, he left London for Windsor, where he spoke to the dean and chapter of Windsor (a church administrator) to petition about Great Hasley Manor. Violet briefly thought he might acquire William Lenthall's manor in the summer of 1660. Violet declared that if the government would not restore the land he lost to him, Violet wanted "Lenthall to pay me the som [*sic*] of Ten Thousand and thirty pounds." Violet brought Charles's alleged letter that promised Violet the estate with him to the dean and chapter of Windsor. Yet the dean did not act on Violet's petition. Now with no hope of landing an estate, Violet briefly thought that he could attempt, again, to prevent fraud at "His Majesty's Mint" but "I have not money" to prosecute the men defrauding the government. In fact, Violet realized that he had no money "To pay my Debts I have contracted for my support since my sequestration."[27] Returning home to London, he felt overwhelmed. Not knowing what else to do, on April 17, 1662, Violet sat down to write a small essay that would be the basis for a last petition to King Charles II asking for his money so that "all my Debts may be fully payd."[28]

This little four-page missive turned into an autobiography. In it, Violet explained the source of his troubles. The first problem, in fact the defining problem of Violet's life, occurred when he was arrested in 1643–44 for carrying Charles I's letter to the merchants of the City of London. Violet wrote that "I undertook to bring up this letter when the Citty [*sic*] was in the height of the madness" of the Civil War. This led to his arrest, caused by the mayor of London, and ultimately cost Violet £20,000. He had never recovered because he could never earn any money after this event. Violet complained that to bring the letter "from the King's father from Oxford to London [in] 1643 shall be my Runie." There was no getting around it. Helping out the Royalist cause had destroyed him.[29]

After explaining that serving the Royalists was the worst financial decision of his life, Violet recalled how his betrayal of the goldsmiths of London in 1634 shaped his subsequent life as well. When he was arrested by Charles I's government in 1634, he was forced to testify against his fellow goldsmiths and his master, Timothy Eman. Violet's suicide attempt at the time, when he swallowed "a dram of mercury" in a bowl of broth, revealed his shame and horror at betraying the man he had lived with for nine years, as well as "the merchants my friends." If his mother, Sara, had not found him and brought him a physician, he might have died. After his twenty-week illness, he realized that God wanted him to proceed. Even though it might have been painful, he resolved to embrace his new role as an informant.[30]

Yet these events paled before the 1643–44 letter episode. Later in the essay, Violet returned to that theme. He writes that it "was against all law to punish a man for bringing a letter from the king." While he was in prison and afterward "to support my Expenses," he had to "borrow great sums of money . . . of my friends." Violet again wished he had his £10,030 from the Lenthall estate to satisfy all of his debts. The debts were not his fault, though, he continued; he incurred them on the king's business. And then continually on the last page, he complains that he needs money—money he had lost because it was stolen from him and lost because he supported the king—to pay his debts. In the closing lines of this little paper, he again repeats himself beseeching the king for "money money will pay debts."

He went with this petition in hand for one last attempt to get money from the king. His goal was to get "all my debts . . . fully payd." It is not clear if anyone in authority ever spoke with him. He was not fully rational at this point and it is unlikely that, even if someone listened to him, he would have made a sympathetic case. Instead, Violet's desperation would have shown through. For only one thought consumed him: fear of debt. Without help, there was no way to pay his creditors.

Disgusted with the world for having failed him and not willing to change his own behavior or imagine a different life, he wanted out. He knew he had one option left. In the opening sentence of his April 17 essay to the king, he said he was "taking a Roman Resolution." During the Renaissance, all things from ancient Rome came back into fashion. This could be rather subversive in Christian society because some classical Roman values clashed with early modern Christian morality. One of the starkest differences was in their view of self-murder. Christians abhorred suicide, while the Romans celebrated it as an honorable exit from life. During the Renaissance, men started emulating the Romans, killing themselves if they saw no honorable continuation of their life. By saying that he was taking a Roman Resolution, Violet was letting his readers know which side of the divide he was on.[31]

On April 20, 1662, after returning from the court in failure, Violet sat at his writing desk one last time at one in the afternoon. His handwriting, always small and usually rather neat, expanded, with only a few lines covering most of a large sheet of paper. His writing was altered because of what he had just done. He wrote, "I have poisoned my self good Lord . . . now the pangs of death are on me I ask Christ Jesus forgiveness forgive me mercy mercy sweet Jesus Pray for me pray for me intercede for me let thy blood wipe away all my sins this great crying sin." He then signed his name the last time, "Tho Violet." Thomas Violet was dead by his own hand.[32]

Even though he was a suicide, Violet asked that he be buried with his parents in St. Katharine Creechurch, a few blocks from his house. For reasons that are not clear, he was. A suicide should not have been buried on church property, but Thomas Violet managed to fool the authorities—perhaps the vicar of the church did not see his last testament. The little building of St. Katharine Creechurch had just been remodeled in 1631. It stands there still, having avoided both the Fire of London in 1666 and German bombs in World War II. In 2017, the church has no permanent congregation because no one lives around it anymore—rather, it is surrounded by commercial buildings. In a historical irony, the Church of England's hierarchy has decreed that the ministry of St. Katharine Creechurch should focus on those who work in commerce, banking, and industry. If any member of the London banking community ever sits in the pews of the church, he or she might glance and see the final resting place of Thomas Violet, whose life is a cautionary tale for anyone in the world of finance.[33]

Although he was dead and buried, Violet's life was not over. His creditors had to fight over his estate. It appears that Alexander Holt and Paul Smith, Violet's cousin, argued over his will. The fact that Smith had written a letter in support of Violet in December 1660 apparently did nothing for him in his cousin's mind, as Violet left everything to Holt. Violet's relationship to his cousin sums up his attitude toward everyone he met. Violet used people when it was convenient for him, but if people could not provide what he wanted, he spurned them and tried to manipulate someone else for his own gain. Smith had failed to deliver to Violet a position or restitution from Charles II's government and so Violet discarded him; Smith did not even warrant a mention in his will. Following Violet's instructions, on July 18, 1663, the probate court gave Violet's estate over to Holt. In the end, Violet's last loyalty was to money, and he gave his to the man to whom he literally owed the most. To Violet, that decision made sense. After all, he valued money above all things.[34]

NOTES

1. Violet, *An Appeal to Caesar*, 47–48.
2. Ibid., 48.
3. *CJ*, vol. 2, 106–7.
4. *CJ*, vol. 3, 136, 353.
5. Violet, *True Discovery of the Commons of England*, 14–15.
6. Rushworth, *Historical Collections*, vol. 5, 379; Violet, *An Appeal to Caesar*, 48; Thomas Violet, *To the Kings Most Excellent Majesty* (London, 1662), 4; *CJ*, vol. 5 322; BL Additional Manuscript 33925, 40r.
7. Thomas Violet, *Two Petitions of Thomas Violet* (London, 1661), 16.
8. Violet, *A Petition against the Jews*, second part, 14.
9. Ibid., 15.
10. Ibid.
11. For Paul Smith, see Geoffrey Smith, *Royalist Agents, Conspirators, and Spies* (Aldershot, UK: Ashgate, 2011), 186, 209.
12. Violet, *A Petition against the Jews*, quotes 20, 22; see also 19–22.
13. Ibid., 19.
14. Ibid., quote 25, 19, 24–25.
15. Ibid., 9.
16. Ibid.,10.
17. Ibid., 4.
18. Ibid., 7.
19. *CSPD, 1661–62*, 12–13.
20. *Calendar of Treasury Books*, vol. 1, 178.
21. *CSPD, 1661–62*, 254.
22. *CSPD, 1660–61*, 249; Wollrych, *Britain in Revolution*, 549, 781.
23. Violet, *An Appeal to Caesar*, 54.

24. Ibid., 13 (mispaginated as 15); Wollrych, *Britain in Revolution*, 780–82.

25. Violet, *A True Narrative of the Proceedings in the Court of Admiraltie*, 122; PROB 20/2650, unpaginated, 3rd document titled "Memorandum."

26. PROB 20/2650, unpaginated, 3rd document titled "Memorandum."

27. Ibid., 1st document, 1st page.

28. Ibid., 2nd page.

29. Ibid.

30. Ibid., 2nd and 3rd pages.

31. See MacDonald and Murphy, *Sleepless Souls*, 86–87, for contemporary views on suicide; and see 174 and 182 for later examples of this belief.

32. PROB 20/2650, unpaginated, 1st document, 4th page.

33. Tony Tucker, *The Visitors Guide to the City of London Churches*, 3rd ed. (London: Guidelines Books & Sales, 2013), 56–57; "Vision Statement," Sanctuary in the City, http://www.sanctuaryinthecity.net/st-katharine/4586821914, accessed May 26, 2017.

34. PROB 11/310/348. For a similar reading of Violet's last days, see Hessayon, "'The Great Trappaner of England,'" 222–24.

Conclusion

For historians, history is in motion. Instead of being absolutely knowable, it is only partially, incompletely comprehensible. Since our understanding of the past constantly changes, historians must always ask how their subject alters other scholars' interpretations of it. For Thomas Violet to be relevant to historians, then, we must recognize what he tells us about seventeenth-century English society and how knowing about his life changes the historiography of the period. Since Violet's life touches on many areas of historical research, we can use Violet to explore a wide range of issues. There are seven areas where Violet can help provide insight into current historiographical debates: (1) the reason people chose sides in the English Civil War; (2) the nature of social relations in early modern London; (3) print culture during the Civil War era; (4) the creation of English nationalism and its links to anti-Semitism; (5) the development of seventeenth-century economic theory; (6) the importance of suicide in early modern English society; and (7) the concept of individualism in early modern Europe.

Throughout the last century, historians debated why individuals decided to support the king or Parliament during the Civil War. In the early decades of the twentieth century, scholars followed the Whig model, which described the war as a struggle between a growing democratic impulse and despotism. For most of the middle of that century, historians were influenced by the Marxist interpretation of the war that claimed that economic factors drove allegiance. According to these historians, merchants and men in towns leaned toward the new bourgeois Parliament, while aristocrats and rural folk supported the king. By the 1970s these views were being challenged by scholars who argued that there was no overarching cause to the war at all. Rather, a series of unforeseen events led to the outbreak of the war. These scholars delighted in revealing how many English people, if they joined a side in the war, did so strictly for personal economic gain. Those who could not make money out of the war often chose to sit it out altogether and avoided picking one side or another. If there were ideological divisions between the combatants, they were the opposite of what the Whigs argued. For instance, instead of the Puritans being the religious revolutionaries, they were actually religious conservatives, fighting against the radical changes in the Church of England that Charles proposed. These historians, called revisionists, were challenged in turn in the 1980s by scholars who claimed that religious and political ideology drove the conflict.

Violet appears at first glance to be a remarkably clear example of an individual who threw his loyalty behind whoever would give him the largest financial reward, lending support to the revisionist interpretation of the conflict. Yet Violet's choice shows how complicated the process of becoming a Royalist or Roundhead could be. If Charles I had not moved against the goldsmiths by trying to take the silver in the Tower and devaluing the currency in 1640, Violet may not have thought that joining the king was such a great opportunity. By alienating the goldsmiths, Charles created an idea in Violet's mind that he could earn money by supporting Charles instead of the goldsmiths, and generate income in a variety of unscrupulous ways. Charles himself would not have been in this position if he had not needed so much money to pay off the Scottish army occupying northern England—something the Scots were only doing because of a religious fight they were having with the king. While Violet then only acted out of selfish motives, he made his choices because of the ideological and tactical choices of major political players. Violet's reactions show that even nonpolitical actors were shaped, whether they liked it or not, by political and religious ideology.[1]

The choice Violet made to become a Royalist was just one of many choices he was afforded because he lived in London. Seventeenth-century London was unlike every other place in England. With hundreds of thousands of residents crowded into only a few square miles, Londoners interacted with more people on a daily basis than someone in a small, rural hamlet might see in a year. The manic energy in the city, combined with the numerous economic, social, and cultural opportunities that the city provided, meant that men enjoyed more freedom there than anywhere else in the British Isles. In 2014, Lynn Hunt argued that in eighteenth-century Britain and France there was a "transition from an embodied self oriented toward equilibrium in . . . emotions to an embodied self looking for increased stimulation and participation in shared spaces, including politics."[2] Hunt identifies globalization, the Enlightenment, and the new opportunities of the eighteenth century as the forces that changed the nature of individuals. The eighteenth century Hunt describes was one Violet would have recognized. Violet wanted to increase the stimulation he experienced and participate in a wide range of activities. He did this by forcing himself into the physical space of people who were his social and economic superiors. His motives were always self-serving, yet his actions—such as when he helped stay the silver ships—could have nationwide repercussions. Violet, a distasteful man who made enemies everywhere, could have such an influence because seventeenth-century London had already experienced the transformation Hunt describes. It was a city that almost demanded that achievements take place in public, shared spaces. For almost a quarter century, Violet took advantage of that by parlaying his sophisticated understanding of currency and gold production into making himself noticed by all the rulers of England.[3]

For Violet, the fly in the ointment was that while he could make various elite actors aware of him, they would rarely do what he wanted. In part this was because early modern England was a hierarchical face-to-face society in which connections determined individuals' chances in all parts of life.[4] Violet, who had few connections and usually severed them at the first opportunity, rarely had the chance to use social networking to help him secure positions. In London, though, someone like Violet, who not only had limited connections but who was also an incredibly unlikable character, could still rise.[5] He managed to do so because of his very specialized skill and his relentless efforts at self-promotion. Violet tried to convince London goldsmiths, King Charles I, the Rump Parliament, Oliver and Richard Cromwell, and King Charles II that he could help them generate money for their respective projects. Violet's ability to reach these powerful men came in a variety of forms. He petitioned them, he spoke to them, he wrote them letters, he bribed their minions, and he sent them printed pamphlets, letters, and documentary evidence.

Violet's use of print helps open insights into the world of print culture. In recent decades, historians have become fascinated by print culture in the early modern period, and in the Civil War era in particular. There are many reasons for this, not least of which is that in the opening decades of the Internet, scholars have wanted to explore a similar time period, when a disruptive technology came and changed how people communicated, learned, spread knowledge, and practiced politics. As Jason Peacey has demonstrated, print culture was a complex beast as a host of actors, including authors, printers, and patrons, interacted in a myriad of ways to produce political and religious tracts as well as news. This process was transformational, as during the Civil War period, readers could use print to learn political and military news, increase their access to information hitherto only available to the elite, and deploy print to shape their own, and their fellows', reactions to political events. When Violet was producing most of his printed petitions—in the 1650s and 1660s—English people had become much more familiar with the printed word than their parents' generation would have been. They were often critical readers of print, and while they found print useful, they also knew enough not to trust everything they read on the printed page.[6]

This phenomenon was what Violet had to deal with when he printed his private petitions. Violet generally did not pay to publish pamphlets for the general reader, but instead he wrote to convince a few members of the elite that he was the winning party in a private economic battle. The genius behind Violet's privately printed petitions was that he was always suggesting that his actions would benefit the state as well as himself. The reason he printed his petitions, after all, was to lobby the state to reward him for services rendered or to hire him so he could earn the state more income. It allowed him to constantly bombard a range of governments with information explaining why his economic policy, or plan to capture silver, would benefit the state's finances. Print allowed Violet to do three things concurrently: (1) contact every significant government employee simultaneously, (2) provide them with large amounts of information and testimonials from a wide range of witnesses, and (3) provide a short summary of that information so that they did not have to read his 150-page tomes.

By closely observing the political climate, Violet could time the publication of his petitions to various leading members of several different versions of the Council of State to stress his ability to help them solve a problem facing them at that particular moment—be it oversight over bullion, better coinage, or a steady supply of silver thread. His petitions were successful, as the Commonwealth and Protectorate governments acted on his advice and requests. The only time printed petitions failed him was after the Restoration, during a time when hundreds of Royalists were demanding some sort of reward from the government. While competing with other Royalists, Violet

suggested that the most important goldsmiths in London be treated as regicides by Charles II and made them hate him even more than they already did.
The combination of relentless competition and enraged enemies meant that
Violet's last printed petitions never amounted to anything. Despite his final
disappointment, the emergence of a widespread print culture in the mid-
seventeenth century gave Violet an opportunity to connect with the most
powerful men in the country in order to influence their behavior. Print, for
Violet, meant he could compensate for his relative unimportance by directly
informing large numbers of important men how he could help their cause.

Violet's private life also sheds light on how the English were simultaneously tolerant of foreigners and xenophobic. This contradiction developed
because in the medieval and early modern period, the English developed a
national identity. Writing about a later time period, Benedict Anderson called
the invention of nationalism the creation of an "imagined community" where
individuals feel powerful connections to people they happen to live with,
rather than just their family.[7] The English embarked on the journey earlier
than other Western Europeans, and their sixteenth- and seventeenth-century
versions of nationalism contained many unifying threads: they were Protestant Christians, they supported property rights, and they fought the Spanish,
who would take these away. While their ideals of political rights were powerful, they also generated a negative description of being English that also
defined them. The English were not Catholic, for instance. They might not
agree on what type of Protestant they were but they knew they were not
Catholic. They were not Jewish. They were not French, Scottish, Dutch, or
Irish. Even people who lived in their own country—the Welsh and the Cornish—they saw as "backward and uncivilized." In fact, one of the reasons
why people fought for Parliament during the English Civil Wars was that the
Royalists seemed to be allied with foreigners.[8]

The result of these developments, where it was sometimes easier to say
what you opposed rather than supported, meant xenophobia was a powerful
tool that united the English. Yet among all this disgust with foreigners and
their different values, England was also a place where immigrants could
come and not only work, but also succeed. Violet was the son of immigrants
who managed to join the Goldsmiths' Company. Further, regular contact
with foreign merchants was a common occurrence for a sizable number of
people in London. The Spanish Jews who pretended to be Catholics lived
unbothered in London for decades, doing business with Englishmen every
day. Even after they announced themselves, the Spanish Jews could be inte-

grated into the community. After all, the parish members of St. Katharine Creechurch rang their church bells for the Spanish Jew Antonio Fernandez Carvajal when he died in 1659. Their action suggests that while the English were creating a national identity that was, in theory, very exclusive and hostile to anyone they perceived as different, in practice they did tolerate people from diverse ethnic and religious backgrounds as their neighbors and business partners. So the rhetoric of the foreigner as enemy, while powerful, did not drive most people's actions.

In times of stress, however, the anti-foreigner, anti-Catholic, and anti-Semitic beliefs propagated in popular culture shattered this usually peaceful coexistence. Violet shows how this worked in all three cases. When trade tensions erupted in the late 1640s and early 1650s with the Dutch, anti-Dutch sentiment grew in England. Fanned by the press, this anger helped start the Anglo-Dutch War from which Violet profited. Anti-Catholicism reared its head during the Irish revolt in the fall of 1641, leading to the crisis that started the English Civil Wars and ended with the English massacres of Irish troops and civilians in Ireland in 1649. Violet, whose Italian-born mother must have been raised Catholic and whose father came from the Catholic part of the Netherlands, felt compelled to use anti-Catholic slurs in his writings to prove his Protestant credentials.

Finally, Violet played a critical role in the movement to drive Jews out of England in the late 1650s and early 1660s. Until recently, Violet's role among English anti-Semites have been underappreciated by historians since scholars tended to focus on the writings of the ministers who opposed the Jewish readmission to England in 1655. While these pamphlets are important, to be sure, they were not as significant as Violet's actions. For Violet did not just debate the merits of allowing the Jews into the country, he actively tried to extort the Jews and expel them. His was not a simple plan, either, but a well thought out, neatly executed, and long-lasting endeavor. If Violet had managed to convince King Charles II that the Jews deserved to be expelled, or if Tobias Knowles had not lost his nerve and sold Violet out, it is very likely that the history of anti-Semitism in England would have ended in 1660 because all of the Jews would have been expelled after having been robbed by Thomas Violet. One reason Violet almost succeeded in his plot was that England's political situation was so unsettled in the late 1650s that anti-Semitism appeared a useful tool to bring the divided nation back together. Clearly, in strained times, the ugly themes that permeated English nationalism not only shaped words, but also actions.[9]

Violet also sheds light on economic history. Violet was one of many thinkers who had had two critical insights about the economy. The first was that free-trade zones actually increased wealth. Violet observed in Dover that when merchants did not have to pay special taxes to trade, they actually brought more trade into a port. This increased employment and the wealth of the surrounding community and it boosted the nation's wealth. Second, Violet's arguments that monopolies hurt consumers resonated with people from all parts of the economic spectrum. Plainly the cost of everything from currants to whale oil was kept artificially high because of companies' monopolies. Many came to agree with this analysis that if there were no more English monopolies, and if foreigners were allowed to move easily through English ports, storing goods there as required, the English would experience a boon in trade, a reduction in the prices of imports, and an increase in income because the policy would require a great many docks, warehouses, manufacturers, and artisans to service the incoming foreign ships.

Violet, though, had the misfortune to connect his argument to the Dutch example (as many other writers had done before him). By supporting the Dutch in the run-up to the Anglo-Dutch War, however, Violet managed to isolate himself from mainstream economic opinion. Consequently, the architects of the Navigation Act ignored his contributions to their legislation, and they did not commission him to support the bill during the war. They disregarded Violet because he chose the wrong time to support the Dutch and because he had actively made it clear that he was a political enemy of the Presbyterians. Since the leaders of the English Republic wanted as much political support as possible, they saw little advantage to allying with a former spy who made enemies every time he participated in a personal or political transaction. Violet's contributions to economic theory were all but forgotten because of his political allegiance and odious personality.[10]

Then there is the troubling issue of Violet's suicide. In their pathbreaking work on suicide in early modern England, Michael MacDonald and Terence R. Murphy made several important insights into the early modern suicide. First of all, during the period from 1500 to 1660 the state spent more time and effort prosecuting suicides than at any time before or after. The penalties were severe. "Self murderers were denied Christian burials. . . . A wooden stake was hammered through the body, pinioning it in the grave, and the hole was filled in. No prayers for the dead were repeated; the ministers did not attend." The suicide's estate was usually sequestered by the state.[11] Of those charged with suicide, the conviction rate was incredibly high: more than 95 percent. [12] Overwhelmingly, elite and common opinion was that suicide was the most heinous crime against God, and that the criminal needed to be punished in all possible ways by the state. However, by the 1650s, several thinkers argued that suicide might not be bad in and of itself. Often inspired by classical writers, they made the case that suicide could be a noble act if necessary. [13] Yet no one suggested that killing oneself over money was noble, even if it was the most common reason why people committed self-murder. [14] Violet's suicide note reveals that he knew about the reemergence of the classical tradition but that as he felt the poison going through his body he did not face death with a Stoic, Roman dispassion. Rather he embraced his Christianity, begging "sweet Jesus" to "intercede for me" and to "wipe away all my sins this great crying sin." Since the word "sin" was the last word he recorded in life, except for his own name, we have here clear and unvarnished evidence that his suicide reconnected with the majority view of his action *after* he already committed the act. As he was dying, Violet was no Roman. Of course, it is also possible to read his last words in another way: even in his last moments, Violet avoided responsibility for his own actions. [15]

Violet spent most of his life ignoring the consequences of his behavior. He could do so because he took advantage of the worst civil war in his nation's history to ingratiate himself with leaders of every government during his country's trial. Despite his many successes, Violet's greed and inability to sympathize with others led to his being called "a sly and dangerous fellow" who would do anything to earn money for himself—no matter who it hurt. His master goldsmith, his neighbors, his mother, families of gold and silver wire drawers, Royalists, Parliamentarians, Jews—all would suffer if he could find a way to extract money from them. [16] Violet only cared for money, and so, like Ebenezer Scrooge before he met his three ghosts, Violet was ready to abuse people to take money from them at every turn. Violet's greed was so immense it blunted his considerable political instincts and his shrewd observations about the business dealings going on in his society. When his unsavory characteristics finally prevented anyone from doing business with him again, he killed himself rather than change his behavior. He never wanted to acknowledge how he hurt others, and at his very end, revealed he did not want to acknowledge how he hurt himself.

Yet Violet got away with it. He apparently was not charged with suicide. And his belongings were not taken by the government. The money that he had left he willed to the creditor he deemed most deserved it. For Violet, this was the best possible ending—he controlled what money he had even after death. In fact, it is likely that his creditors' need for recompense from Violet's estate may have been why he was never charged with suicide.[17] If that is true, it is ironic that Violet's selfishness actually prevented something bad from happening to his creditors. For if there was one constant in his life, it was self-centeredness. On the one hand, this made him remarkably industrious. It spurred him to lobby kings, noblemen, the Council of State, merchants, foreigners, and generals. He was ready to attempt business deals that would have intimidated the most successful goldsmith. His economic writings were insightful and, in the main, helpful to English policy makers. Yet on the other hand, his selfishness made him a loathsome character. If he could turn a profit by betraying them, Violet shamelessly would turn his back on someone he had allied himself with. He always went into a business deal with the idea that he would gain at someone else's expense. He held grudges for decades and he blamed other people for his own misfortune, even though he never acknowledged how he ruined other people. Violet never felt sorry for ruining the Symonds brothers and he never stopped hating Wollaston for his role in arresting Violet. Violet's complete disregard for others comes out in his suicide note when he asks for God's forgiveness for his sin—of suicide—not for his uncountable sins in life. By avoiding all responsibility for his actions, he reveals what his suicide was—a final selfish act to avoid paying the price for his narcissism.

Violet's narcissism defined him because he lived in an era in which individuals could create their own lives. The growth of individualism was a real phenomenon in early modern Europe. Scholars are right to point out that various Europeans managed to invent themselves in a way that would not have been possible before. While no one could live a life unconnected to others during this period, their actions laid the groundwork, after the Enlightenment and Industrial Revolution, for most Europeans to see individual happiness, success, and fulfillment as the ultimate goal in the human experience. Seventeenth-century Londoners would have recognized some of these ideas, as many of them strove to create their own sense of identity. Violet did this more than most, as he actively made his own way in the world without regard for social custom or convention. Yet Violet's path to individual fulfillment always came at a cost to others. He did what he wanted in order to scam, fine, demean, or manipulate others into giving him money and power. Violet created himself, but the end product was despicable. He teaches us that the new world of individualism Europeans developed allowed humans to produce a society where individuals had more rights and opportunities, but were free to use them to damage others and live completely selfishly. Violet did that, and the cost for him was that he died alone, by his own hand, mourned by no one.[18]

St. Katharine Creechurch, Violet's parish church and where he apparently was buried, stands in central London today, the same building Violet walked through in life. I hope that you have a chance to visit St. Katharine Creechurch, as it is almost the only surviving example of a church built in the 1630s in the city. While not as famous as Christopher Wren's churches, the church manages to be both stately and intimate. Even for the nonreligious, the calm of the interior and the beautiful music of the choirs that sing there is a relief after walking the streets of modern London. I have to say, though, that I have wondered, as I have sat inside St. Katharine Creechurch on a dreary winter's day, if Thomas Violet was still wandering the pews, carrying chains of his own making.

NOTES

1. See Ronald Hutton, *Debates in Stuart History* (Basingstoke, UK: Palgrave Macmillan, 2004), 6–31, for an overview of the historiography; the literature on taking sides in the Civil Wars is substantial. For constitutional reasons for choosing sides, see Barbara Donagan, "Casuistry and Allegiance in the English Civil War," in *Writing and Political Engagement in Seventeenth-Century England*, eds. Derek Hirst and Richard Strier (Cambridge: Cambridge University Press, 1999), 90–91. For local reasons, see David Underdown, *Revel, Riot and Rebellion: Popular Politics and Culture in England 1603–1660* (Oxford: Oxford University Press, 1985); Anne Hughes, *Politics, Society and Civil War in Warwickshire, 1620–1660* (Cambridge: Cambridge University Press, 1987); Mark Stoyle, *Loyalty and Locality: Popular Allegiance in Devon during the English Civil War* (Exeter, UK: University of Exeter Press, 1994). For religious reasons, see John Morrill, "The Religious Context of the English Civil War," *Transactions of the Royal Historical Society* 34 (1984): 157. For a description of the fluidity of choosing sides, see Braddick, *God's Fury, England's Fire*, 233, 236.

2. Lynn Hunt, *Writing History in a Global Era* (New York: W. W. Norton, 2014), 134.

3. For a depiction of London and England at the start of the Civil War and its public sphere, see David Cressy, *England on Edge: Crisis and Revolution 1640–1642* (Oxford: Oxford University Press, 2006), passim.

4. See Anna Bayman, *Thomas Dekker and the Culture of Pamphleteering in Early Modern London* (Farnham, UK: Ashgate, 2014), 67–88, for a wonderful description of early modern London.

5. See Cressy, *England on Edge*, 347–76, for a description of the social order and how it was challenged during the lead-up to the Civil War.

6. Peacey, *Politicians and Pamphleteers: Propaganda During the English Civil Wars and Interregnum*. See Peacey, *Print and Public Politics in the English Revolution*, passim, for the public uses of print, 14–18, for how it changed English society. While the literature about print culture is growing rapidly, the best places to start exploring these debates are in Peacey's works

and Adam Fox, *Oral and Literate Culture in England, 1500–1700* (Oxford: Oxford University Press, 2000).

7. Benedict Anderson, *Imagined Communities: Reflections on the Origin and Spread of Nationalism*, rev. ed. (London: Verso, 1983, 2006), 6.

8. Stoyle, *Soldiers and Strangers*, 1–8, quotes on 3, 8. For a good overview of English nationalism in a comparative context, start with Adrian Hastings, *The Construction of Nationhood: Ethnicity, Religion and Nationalism* (Cambridge: Cambridge University Press, 1997). See also Yerby, *The English Revolution and the Roots of Environmental Change*, 176–84, for a good description of the development of the idea of English liberty.

9. Julius, *Trials of the Diaspora: A History of Anti-Semitism in England*, 248–51; Katz, *The Jews in the History of England*, 134–42; Hessayon, "'The Great Trappaner of England,'" 217–22.

10. See Pincus, *Protestantism and Patriotism*, 11–14, 40–50, for a summary of the historiography on the Anglo-Dutch War. For a persuasive exploration of the economists whose ideas did influence policy, see Carl Wennerlind, *Casualties of Credit: The English Financial Revolution, 1620–1720* (Cambridge, MA: Harvard University Press, 2011), 44–79.

11. MacDonald and Murphy, *Sleepless Souls*, 15.

12. Ibid., 16.

13. Ibid., 86–88.

14. Ibid., 270.

15. PROB 20/2650, 1st document, 4th page.

16. Violet, *An Appeal to Caesar*, 54.

17. See Paul Seaver, ed., *The History of Suicide in England, 1650–1850*, vol. 1 (London: Routledge, 2012), xxxiii–xxxv, for reasons why the government dramatically reduced the number of criminal convictions against suicides.

18. For a nice description of the ability to self-fashion in the early modern period, read the following debate between Robert Finlay and Natalie Zemon Davis: Robert Finlay, "The Refashioning of Martin Guerre," *American Historical Review* 93, no. 3 (June 1988): 553–71; Natalie Zemon Davis, "On the Lame," *American Historical Review* 93, no. 3 (June 1988): 572–603.

Bibliography

PRIMARY SOURCES

Manuscript Locations

British Library (BL)
BL Additional Manuscript 33925
BL Harley Manuscript (MS) 6034
National Archives, Records of the Prerogative Court of Canterbury (PROB)
PROB 20/2650
PROB 11/310/348

Printed Sources

Anon. *The Great Trappanner of England Discovered.* London, 1660.
Ben Israel, Menasseh. *The Hope of Israel.* London, 1652.
———. *Menasseh ben Israel's Mission to Oliver Cromwell: Being a Reprint of the Pamphlets Published by Menasseh ben Israel to Promote the Re-Admission of the Jews to England, 1649–1656.* Edited by Lucien Wolf. London: Macmillan, 1901.
Calendar of State Papers Domestic (CSPD).
Calendar of Treasury Books.
Dury, John. *A Case of Conscience, Whether it be lawful to Admit Jews into a Christian Commonwealth?* London, 1656.
Journals of the House of Commons (CJ).
Journals of the House of Lords (LJ).
[Jessey, H., attrib. author]. *A narrative of the Late Proceeds at White-Hall.* London, 1656.
"Navigation Act." In *The Constitutional Documents of the Puritan Revolution, 1625–1660*, 3rd ed., edited by S. R. Gardiner, 468–71. Oxford: Oxford University Press, 1906.
Pepys, Samuel. *The Diary of Samuel Pepys: A Selection.* Edited by Robert Latham. London: Penguin Books, 1985.

Prideaux, Walter. *Memorials of the Goldsmiths' Company*. London: Worshipful Company of Goldsmiths, 1896.

Pym, John. "A Commons Debate of the Trade Depression, Recorded by John Pym, 26 February, 1621." In *Seventeenth-Century Economic Documents*, edited by Joan Thirsk and J. P. Cooper, 1–2. Oxford: Oxford University Press, 1972.

Rushworth, John. *Historical Collections*. Vol. 2. London: n.p., 1721.

Smith, Adam. *The Wealth of Nations*. 1776. Reprint, New York: Bantam Dell, 2003.

St. George, Sir Henry. *The Visitation of London, Anno Domini 1633, 1634, 1635*. Edited by Joseph Jackson Howard. London: Harleian Society, 1880.

———. *The Visitation of London, Anno Domini 1633, 1634, 1635*. Edited by Joseph Jackson Howard. London: Harleian Society, 1883.

"The Solemn League and Covenant." In *The Constitutional Documents of the Puritan Revolution, 1625–1660*, 3rd ed., edited by S. R. Gardiner, 267–71. Oxford: Oxford University Press, 1906.

Thurloe, John. *A Collection of State Papers of John Thurloe*. London: n.p., 1742.

Violet, Thomas. *The Advancement of Merchandize*. London, [17 Feb.] 1651.

———. *The Answer of the Corporation of Moniers in the Mint*. London, 1653.

———. *An Appeal to Caesar*. London, 1662.

———. *An Humble Declaration to the Right Honourable the Lord and Commons in Parliament Assembled*. London, 1643.

———. *A Petition against the Jews*. London, 1661.

———. *Proposal Humbly Presented to His Highness Oliver*. London, 1656.

———. *To his Highness*. London, 1656.

———. *To the Kings Most Excellent Majesty*. London, 1662.

———. *To the Right Honourable the Lords in Parliament Assembled*. London, 1660.

———. *To the Supreme Authority the Parliament of England*. London, 1660.

———. *A True Discovery to the Commons of England*. London, 1650.

———. *A True Narrative of Som remarkable Proceedings*. London, 1653.

———. *A True Narrative of som remarkable-Procedings concerning the ships Samson, Salvadore and George*. London, 1653.

———. *A True Narrative of the Proceedings in the Court of Admiraltie*. London, 1659.

———. *Two Petitions of Thomas Violet*. London, 1661.

Worsley, Benjamin. *The Advocate*. London, Aug. 1652.

———. *Free Ports, the Nature and Necessitie of them Stated*. London, 1652.

Wortley, Francis. "A Loyall Song" ([16 Sept.] 1647). In *Political Ballads Published in England during the Commonwealth*, vol. 3, edited by Thomas Wright. London: Percey Society, 1841, 97.

SECONDARY SOURCES

Anderson, Benedict. *Imagined Communities: Reflections on the Origin and Spread of Nationalism*. Rev. ed. 1983. Rev. ed., London: Verso, 2006.

Appleby, Joyce Oldham. *Economic Thought and Ideology in Seventeenth-Century England*. Princeton, NJ: Princeton University Press, 1978.

Bayman, Anna. *Thomas Dekker and the Culture of Pamphleteering in Early Modern London*. Farnham, UK: Ashgate, 2014.

Braddick, Michael. *God's Fury, England's Fire: A New History of the English Civil Wars*. London: Allen Lane, 2008.

Brenner, Robert. *Merchants and Revolution: Commercial Change, Political Conflict, and London's Oversees Traders, 1550–1653*. Cambridge: Cambridge University Press, 1993.

Brigden, Susan. *New Worlds, Lost Worlds: The Rule of the Tudors*. London: Penguin Books, 2000.

Bucholz, Robert, and Newton Key. *Early Modern England, 1485–1714: A Narrative History*. 2nd ed. Singapore: Wiley-Blackwell, 2009.

Challis, C. E. "Lord Hastings to the Great Silver Recoinage, 1464–1699." In *A New History of the Royal Mint*, edited by C. E. Challis, 179–397. Cambridge: Cambridge University Press, 1992.

Cressy, David. *England on Edge: Crisis and Revolution 1640–1642*. Oxford: Oxford University Press, 2006.

Davis, Natalie Zemon. "On the Lame." *American Historical Review* 93, no. 3 (June 1988): 572–603.

Donagan, Barbara. "Casuistry and Allegiance in the English Civil War." In *Writing and Political Engagement in Seventeenth-Century England*, edited by Derek Hirst and Richard Strier, 89–111. Cambridge: Cambridge University Press, 1999.

Farnell, J. E. "The Navigation Act of 1651, the First Dutch War, and the London Merchant Community." *Economic History Review* 16, no. 3 (1964): 439–54.

Finlay, Robert. "The Refashioning of Martin Guerre." *American Historical Review* 93, no. 3 (June 1988): 553–71.

Fox, Adam. *Oral and Literate Culture in England, 1500–1700*. Oxford: Oxford University Press, 2000.

Gardiner, S. R. *History of the Great Civil War 1642–1649*. London: Longmans, Green, 1886.

——. *History of the Great Civil War 1642–1649*. London: Longmans, Green, 1889.

——. *History of the Great Civil War 1642–1649*. London: Longmans, Green, 1894.

Gardiner, S. R., ed. *The Constitutional Documents of the Puritan Revolution, 1625–1660*. 3rd ed. Oxford: Oxford University Press, 1906.

Glover, Elizabeth. *The Gold & Silver Wyre-Drawers*. London: Phillimore, 1979.

Hastings, Adrian. *The Construction of Nationhood: Ethnicity, Religion and Nationalism*. Cambridge: Cambridge University Press, 1997.

Hessayon, Ariel. "'The Great Trappaner of England': Thomas Violet, Jews and crypto-Jews during the English Revolution and at the Restoration." In *The Experience of Revolution in Stuart Britain and Ireland*, edited by Michael J. Braddick and David L. Smith, 210–30. Cambridge: Cambridge University Press, 2011.

Hughes, Ann. *Gangraena and the Struggle for the English Revolution*. Oxford: Oxford University Press, 2004.

——. *Politics, Society and Civil War in Warwickshire, 1620–1660*. Cambridge: Cambridge University Press, 1987.

Hunt, Lynn. *Writing History in a Global Era*. New York: W. W. Norton, 2014.

Hutton, Ronald. *Debates in Stuart History*. Basingstoke, UK: Palgrave Macmillan, 2004.

——. *The Restoration*. Oxford: Oxford University Press, 1986.

Israel, Jonathan. *Dutch Primacy in World Trade, 1585–1740*. Cambridge: Cambridge University Press, 1989.

Julius, Anthony. *Trials of the Diaspora: A History of Anti-Semitism in England*. Oxford: Oxford University Press, 2010.

Katz, David. *The Jews in the History of England 1485–1850*. Oxford: Oxford University Press, 1994.

——. *Philo-Semitism and the Readmission of the Jews to England 1603–1655*. Oxford: Oxford University Press, 1982.

Kishlansky, Mark. *A Monarchy Transformed: Britain 1603–1714*. London: Penguin Books, 1996.

Lasch, Christopher. *The Culture of Narcissism*. New York: W. W. Norton, 1978.

Leng, Thomas. *Benjamin Worsley (1618–1677): Trade, Interest, and the Spirit in Revolutionary England*. Woodbridge, UK: Royal Historical Society, 2008.

Lindley, Keith. *Popular Politics and Religion in Civil War London*. Aldershot, UK: Scholar Press, 1997.

MacDonald, Michael, and Terence R. Murphy. *Sleepless Souls: Suicide in Early Modern England*. Oxford: Oxford University Press, 1990.

McElligott, Jason. *Royalism, Print and Censorship in Revolutionary England*. Woodbridge, UK: Boydell Press, 2007.

Morrill, John. "The Religious Context of the English Civil War." *Transactions of the Royal Historical Society* 34 (1984): 155–78.

Ormond, David. *The Rise of Commercial Empires: England and the Netherlands in the Age of Mercantilism, 1650–1770*. Cambridge: Cambridge University Press, 2003.

Peacey, Jason. *Politicians and Pamphleteers: Propaganda During the English Civil Wars and Interregnum*. Aldershot, UK: Ashgate, 2004.

———. *Print and Public Politics in the English Revolution*. Cambridge: Cambridge University Press, 2013.

Pincus, Steven. *Protestantism and Patriotism: Ideologies and the Making of English Foreign Policy, 1650–1688*. Cambridge: Cambridge University Press, 1996.

Raymond, Joad. *The Invention of the Newspaper: English Newsbooks 1641–1649*. Oxford: Oxford University Press, 1996.

Sabean, David. *Power in the Blood*. Cambridge: Cambridge University Press, 1988.

Seaver, Paul, ed. *The History of Suicide in England, 1650–1850*. London: Routledge, 2012.

Sharpe, Kevin. *The Personal Rule of Charles I*. New Haven, CT: Yale University Press, 1992.

Smith, Geoffrey. *Royalist Agents, Conspirators, and Spies*. Aldershot, UK: Ashgate, 2011.

Smith, Lacey Baldwin. *This Realm of England 1399–1688*. 8th ed. New York: Houghton Mifflin, 2001.

Spufford, Peter. *Power and Profit: The Merchant in Medieval Europe*. New York: Thames and Hudson, 2002.

Stearns, Peter, and Carol Stearns, eds. *Emotion and Social Change: Toward a New Psychohistory*. New York: Holmes & Meier, 1988.

Stoyle, Mark. *Loyalty and Locality: Popular Allegiance in Devon during the English Civil War*. Exeter, UK: University of Exeter Press, 1994.

———. *Soldiers & Strangers: An Ethnic History of the English Civil War*. New Haven, CT: Yale University Press, 2005.

Tubb, Amos. "Independent Presses: The Politics of Print in England During the Late 1640s." *Seventeenth Century* 27, no. 3 (Autumn 2012): 287–312.

Tucker, Tony. *The Visitors Guide to the City of London Churches*. 3rd ed. London: Guidelines Books & Sales, 2013.

Underdown, David. *Revel, Riot and Rebellion: Popular Politics and Culture in England 1603–1660*. Oxford: Oxford University Press, 1985.

"Vision Statement." Sanctuary in the City, 2015. http://www.sanctuaryinthecity.net/stkatharine/4586821914. Accessed May 26, 2017.

Ward, A. W., G. W. Prothero, and Stanley Leathes, eds. *The Cambridge Modern History Atlas*. Cambridge: Cambridge University Press, 1924.

Wennerlind, Carl. *Casualties of Credit: The English Financial Revolution, 1620–1720*. Cambridge, MA: Harvard University Press, 2011.

————. "Money: Hartlibian Political Economy and the New Culture of Credit." In *Mercantilism Reimagined: Political Economy in Early Modern Britain and Its Empire*, edited by Philip J. Stern and Carl Wennerlind, 74–93. Oxford: Oxford University Press, 2014.

Woolrych, Austin. *Britain in Revolution: 1625–1660*. Oxford: Oxford University Press, 2002.

Yerby, George. *The English Revolution and the Roots of Environmental Change: The Changing Concept of the Land in Early Modern England*. New York: Routledge, 2016.

REFERENCES

Dictionary of National Biography (DNB)
English Short Title Catalog (ESTC)
Oxford English Dictionary (OED)

Index

Act of Indemnity, 110
Act of Oblivion, 66
Admiralty Court, 91–98
The Advancement of Merchandize: or Certain Propositions for the Improvement of the Trade of this Commonwealth to the Right Honorable the Council of State (Violet), 55–61, 68–72, 80–81
The Advocate (Worsley), 71
Alderman. *See* Wollaston, John
Amery, Robert, 30–31, 33
Amsterdam, Netherlands, 69, 91, 96–97, 98
Anglo-Dutch War, 122, 138, 139; Blake influencing, 88–89; English Channel in, 88–89; First, 71, 87–102, 108; treasure ships influenced by, 87–102; Tromp influencing, 88–89
anti-Catholicism, 4, 114–116, 138
anti-Semitism, 4, 105–116, 138
Antwerp, Netherlands, 9
Appleby, Joyce Oldham, 58, 73n9
Archer, Francis, 30–31
Arminianism, 39–40
army, 83–85, 99–100, 102, 117n25
Assessment, 44
Athias, Moses, 109–110
attorney general. *See* Bankes, John

Bankes, John, 23, 24, 26, 28

Barebones' Parliament, 100
Battle Hall, 35–36, 50
Battle of Dunbar, 62
Belgium, 98
ben Israel, Menasseh, 107–109
Blake, Robert, 88–89
Blondeau, Pierre, 105
Boschaert, George, 100
Bradbourn, Edward, 33–34
Bradshaw, John, 67–68, 72, 80–81, 95–97, 101, 122
Brook, Basil, 45–50
Burlamacke, Philip, 97

Cadiz, Spain, 90
Cage, Philip, 35–36, 50
Calais, France, 13, 91, 98
Calendrine, Pompey, 97
Calvinists, 47. *See also* Presbyterians
cardecus, 13, 15–18
Carlisle (lord), 33–34
Carvajal, Antonio, 105–112, 114–116, 138
Carvajal, Maria, 114
Catholics, 39–42, 56–57, 62, 106–107, 137–138. *See also* anti-Catholicism
charges, 36n2
Charles I (king), 99, 133–134; during anti-Semitic period, 112; coins influenced by, 28–29, 43–44, 119, 124–125; Common Hall message presentation, 49; economist period and, 53–55, 59,

151

61–62, 67–68, 73n5; English Civil War
    influencing, 3, 39–50, 53–55, 61–62,
    67–68, 73n5, 77; execution influencing,
    42, 62; during goldsmith period, 15–20;
    Goldsmiths' Hall information, 49–50;
    interrogation, 49–50; letters, 48–50,
    54–55, 120–121, 129; overview, 2, 3;
    spy period influenced by, 23–35;
    Wollaston, J., influencing, 77, 78. *See
    also* Royalists
Charles II (king), 112; general pardon of,
    127; Haseley Manor recommendation
    of, 125; Lenthall influenced by, 125,
    129; letter of, 128; petitions to, 2,
    113–116, 119–131, 135–137, 138;
    servants asked by, 121–122; Smith
    asked by, 122–124; story told to,
    119–124, 129–131
Cheapside Street, 18–19
Church of England, 130, 134
clipping, 11–12, 64, 67, 78–83, 105
coal, 68
coins, 2; Charles I influencing, 28–29,
    43–44, 119, 124–125; counterfeiting,
    105–112; during economist period,
    59–61, 63–64, 64–67, 69–70; Roman
    resolution influenced by, 119, 124–125;
    during Royalist period, 43–44; during
    spy period, 28–29. *See also* goldsmiths;
    Royal Mint
Coke, John, 16–20, 23, 24, 27–28, 59
Commissioners of Dutch Prize Goods, 91
Commission for Prize Goods, 91, 98
Committee on Foreign Affairs, 97
Common Hall, 49
Commonwealth, 136; in economist period,
    62–72; enemies faced by, 62; New
    Model Army, 61–62; during republican
    period, 91–102; Roman resolution and,
    119, 121–124, 126, 127; during
    trappaner period, 80–83
confession, 16–18
conspiracy, 45–50
Cooper, J. P., 74n54
Corbet, John, 100–101, 120
Cornish, 137
Council of State, 136; during anti-Semitic
    period, 110–112; during economist
    period, 64–72; during goldsmith period,

15, 18; Medcalfe protesting to, 18;
    during republican period, 87–100, 101;
    Roman resolution influenced by, 121,
    122–124; during spy period, 24–28,
    32–33, 34; during trappaner period, 79,
    80–83; treasure ships impounded by,
    87–100, 101
counterfeiting, 105–112
coup, 84–85, 98–99, 122–124
Courtney, William, 114
Court of Admiralty, 91–98
Court of Assistants, 26–28
Creechurch Lane, 109
Cromwell, Oliver: during anti-Semitic
    period, 105, 108–109, 113, 115–116;
    Battle of Dunbar won by, 62; during
    economist period, 62; during republican
    period, 97–102; Roman resolution
    influenced by, 119, 121–124, 125;
    Scots defeated by, 62; during trappaner
    period, 84–85; treasure ships
    influencing, 97–102
Cromwell, Richard, 101–102
Crosse, Thomas, 18–19
Crowe, Sackville, 97
culling. *See* clipping
currants, 60
Customs Board, 124–125

Davis, Thomas, 121–122
death, 1. *See also* suicide
debtors' prison, 128
Dickens, Charles, 2
Digby, George, 48–50
Dives, Lewis, 55
Dorset (earl), 34
Dover, England, 139; during economist
    period, 59, 60–61, 64, 66–67; during
    goldsmith period, 13; during republican
    period, 89, 90; Roman resolution
    influenced by, 120, 122
Dugard, William, 68, 102
Dutch, 78; during anti-Semitic period,
    107–109; ben Israel as, 107–109;
    during economist period, 57, 63–64, 65,
    66–67, 69–72, 139; goldsmith and,
    9–10, 11; overview, 138, 139; during
    republican period, 87–102; Roman
    resolution influenced by, 120, 122–123,

124; during Royalist period, 40–41, 43–44; treasure ships, 87–102, 122–124, 135

Dyamont, Sara. *See* Vyolett, Sara

East India Company, 58, 59, 113, 124

"Ebenezer Scrooge" (fictional character), 2, 140

economist, 53–72, 72n3, 139, 141

economy, 2, 3, 5–6, 133–135, 139, 141; anti-Semitic period and, 105, 113–116; Appleby on, 73n9; goldsmiths shaping, 10, 12, 20; Jews threatening, 113–116; pamphlets, 58, 67–72, 79–83, 105, 121–125, 136–137; Royalist period, 39–50; during spy period, 25–28; strategies, 39–50, 119–125, 136–137; during trappaner period, 79–83; Wollaston hurting, 79–83. *See also* free trade; monopolies

Edward I, 114

Elizabeth I (queen), 18

Eman, Timothy, 2, 11–13, 16–17, 24, 129

England. *See specific topics*

English Channel, 88–89

English Civil Wars. *See specific topics*

English nationalism, 4, 137–138

English Republic, 139; Admiralty Court, 91–98; during anti-Semitic period, 107–113, 117n25; during economist period, 62–72; Jews influenced by, 107–113; navy, 88–102; during republican period, 87–102; Roman resolution influenced by, 119, 121–124, 126, 127; treasure ships impounded by, 87–102. *See also* Commonwealth

essay to King Charles II, 128–131

Essex county, 35–36, 61, 64, 121

ethnic cleansing, 42–43

Europe, 69, 87–88, 89–102

Exchange, 25–28

execution, 42, 62

Fernando, Anthony. *See* Carvajal, Antonio

Fire of London, 130

First Anglo-Dutch War, 71, 87–102, 108

First Bishops' War, 41

fishermen, 56–57

Flanders, 63–64

Flutter, Henry, 12–13, 14, 16–17, 19–20, 24

foreigners: during anti-Semitic period, 106–112, 113–116; during economist period, 65; during goldsmith period, 10, 12–13; overview, 4; Royalist period influenced by, 46–48; shopkeepers trading with, 65; spy period influenced by, 24. *See also* free trade; xenophobia

fortune, 21n10

France, 13, 15–18, 19–20, 40, 134–135. *See also* Calais, France

Free Ports, the Nature and Necessitie of them Stated (Worsley), 72

free quarter, 65–66

free trade, 5–6, 73n12, 139; during economist period, 55–61, 65, 66–67, 68–72; during spy period, 27–28

French, 40–41, 60–61, 120; Blondeau as, 105; during goldsmith period, 13, 15–18, 19–20; during spy period, 23–24, 32–33

Gares, 33

general pardon, 127

gentry, 35–36, 113

George, Otho, 94, 97–98

Germany, 90–102, 122

Gibbs, Richard, 31–33

Gibs, William, 24

God, 4–5, 17, 36, 47, 57, 83 85; during anti-Semitic period, 107–108, 112, 114, 115–116; Roman resolution influenced by, 123–124, 129, 140, 141

gold, 5, 24–36, 43–44, 49, 75–85, 135; during anti-Semitic period, 106, 113, 114, 115; during economist period, 60, 65, 68; during republican period, 93–94, 99, 102; Roman resolution influenced by, 119–120, 121, 124–125, 126. *See also* goldsmiths; wire drawers

Gold and Silver Wire Drawers' Company, 28–29, 31–33

Golden Age, 63–64

goldsmith period, 9–20

goldsmiths, 2, 9–20, 23–36, 102, 134, 136–137; during economist period, 55, 68; Roman resolution and, 125–128, 129; during Royalist period, 40, 43, 44,

45–50; troy ounce used by, 85n12. *See also* Eman, Timothy; Wollaston, John
Goldsmiths' Company, 10–20, 20n4, 25–29, 75, 137
Goldsmiths' Hall, 14, 26–28, 49–50
gold trade, spy on, 23–36
Gravesend, England, 122
Great Hasley Manor, 125, 128
great ones, 92
Green, Edward, 75
Green, Rebecca. *See* Wollaston, Rebecca
Green, William, 33
Greenland Company, 60, 70
Guerdain, Aaron, 79, 81, 82–83

Hamburg, Germany, 90–102, 122
Hampton Court, 54–55, 73n5
Harrison, Thomas, 98
Haseley Manor, 125, 128
Haselrig, Arthur, 48, 120
Hebrew, 107
Henrietta-Maria (queen), 25, 33–34
Henry VIII (king), 15, 18
Holland. *See* Netherlands
Holland (earl), 24–28
Holt, Alexander, 102, 128, 131
House of Commons, 68; during Royalist period, 42, 44, 47–48, 48; Spanish ambassador going to, 94; during trappaner period, 78–79, 80
House of Lords, 42
Hunt, Lynn, 134–135

Independents, 67–68, 79, 83–84, 108
individualism, 3, 6, 133–135, 137, 141–142
Internet, 135–136
Interregnum, 123
interrogation, 49–50
interrogations, 16–18
Ireland, 62, 65, 83, 138
Irish, 39, 42–43, 62, 65, 138
Italian Renaissance, 4–5, 6, 130

James I, 42
Jenkins (judge), 72n3
Jesus Christ, 1, 108–109, 115–116, 130, 140

Jews, 2, 4, 102, 105–116, 119, 137–138, 138
joint stock companies, 59, 63
The Journal of the House of Commons, 78

King of Spain, 96–97
King's Bench jail, 45–48, 61, 120, 121
Kirk, 47
Knowles, Tobias, 110–112, 138

Lambert, John, 98
landed gentry, 35–36
Leadenhall Street, 10
Lee. *See* Read
Lenthall, William, 125, 128, 129
letters, 48–50, 54–55, 100, 120–121, 128–129
liberty, 3, 4, 6, 65
Lombard Street, 11–20
London, England. *See specific topics*
Long Parliament, 41–43
Lord Mayor. *See* Wollaston, John
Lost Tribes of Israel, 107
Lubeck, Germany, 90, 97

MacDonald, Michael, 139–140
Man in Moon. *See* Riley, Theophilus
Marranos, 107–116
Marxist interpretation, 133–134
massacres, 42–43, 138
Master of Mint, 76, 79, 81–83. *See also* Wollaston, John
Medcalfe, Oswald, 18, 19
melter, 78–83
Mercantile System, 5
merchants, 106–116, 133–134, 137–139; during economist period, 55, 56–61, 71; during goldsmith period, 12, 13, 19–20; during republican period, 88, 89, 89–102; Roman resolution influenced by, 120–125, 127–128, 129–130; during Royalist period, 40–41, 43–44, 45–50; spy period influencing, 23–24; during trappaner period, 79, 80–83. *See also* free trade; goldsmiths; trade
Merchant Strangers, 70
Middle Ages, 40, 56, 114
mint. *See* Royal Mint
Monck, George, 112–113

Monk (general), 100

monopolies, 5, 139; East India Company, 58, 59, 113, 124; during economist period, 59–60, 70–72; Greenland Company, 60, 70; Muscovy Company, 60, 70; Navigation Act cutting into, 88; during republican period, 88; during spy period, 28, 29; trappaner period influenced by, 75–83; Turkey Company, 60, 70; Virginia Company, 59

Moorish mother, 10

Mordant, Charles, 35–36

Mun, Thomas, 58, 65

Murphy, Terence R., 139–140

Muscovy Company, 60, 70

name, spelling of, 11, 20n4

narcissism, 141

nationalism, 4, 137–138

Native Americans, 107

Navigation Act, 70–72, 87–88, 139

navy, 88–102

Negro privateer, 89

Netherlands, 122, 138; during anti-Semitic period, 108; during economist period, 66, 69; during republican period, 87–102; during Royalist period, 43–44; Spanish, 9; treasure ships, 87–102, 122–124, 135; Vyolett, P., born in, 9. *See also* Dutch

Newcastle, England, 68

New England, 47

New Model Army, 61–62

newsbooks, 88

noble lady (unnamed), 33–34

Nominated Assembly, 100

non-Protestants, 4

oil, 60

Old Bailey, 111

Old Testament, 107

old White, 54

Ostend, Belgium, 98

Ottoman Empire, 60

Oxford, England, 42, 46–49, 77, 129

Painter, Humphrey, 121–122

Palmer, Andrew, 30–31

pamphlets, 4, 85n1, 100, 111–112, 126; economy, 58, 67–72, 79–83, 105, 121–125, 136–137; Jews, 107–109, 138

pardon, 125, 127

Parliament, 2, 133–134, 137; anti-Semitic period influenced by, 108, 110–112, 114–116; economist period influenced by, 53–62, 64–72; during republican period, 87–102; Roman resolution and, 119–124, 125, 126; during royalist period, 39–50; during trappaner period, 76, 77, 78–85; treasure ships impounded by, 87–102; Wollaston, J., petitioning, 77. *See also* House of Commons; Rump Parliament

Parliamentarians. *See* Roundheads

Parliament of Paris, 19–20

Patton Hall, 35–36, 50

Peacey, Jason, 136, 142n6

Personal Rule, 40–41

Peter's House jail, 120

petitions, 2, 4; during anti-Semitic period, 109, 111–112, 113–116, 138; to Charles II, 2, 113–116, 119–131, 135–137, 138; during economist period, 64–67, 68; during goldsmith period, 18–19; during republican period, 92, 98, 100–102; Roman resolution influenced by, 119–131; during Royalist period, 45, 48–50; during spy period, 28–36; during trappaner period, 77, 78–79, 80–83, 84–85

Pickering, George, 31–33

pieces of 8, 65

Pight, Richard, 105–112, 119

poison, 1, 17, 49–50, 130, 139–142

Presbyterians, 139; during anti-Semitic period, 109, 112–113; during economist period, 57, 61–62, 67–68, 72; during republican period, 96; during Royalist period, 39–44, 47–48; during trappaner period, 77, 83–85. *See also* Wollaston, John

Pride, Thomas, 62, 68

print, 3–4, 68–72, 88, 102, 135–137, 142n6. *See also* pamphlets

Privy Council, 15, 114

protectionism, 5–6

Protectorate, 121–124, 127, 136

Protestant Reformation, 6, 107
Protestants, 4, 6, 39–43, 88, 106, 137, 138
Puritans, 41, 42, 47, 77, 108, 134
Pym, John, 47–48

Ramadg, David, 121–122
Read (colonel), 45–50
refiners, 28–29, 30, 49–50, 60–61
Reformation, 6, 107
regicides, 112, 136–137
Registrar and Searcher of Gold and Silver,
    113
Renaissance, 4–5, 6, 130
republican, 87–102
Restoration, 2–3, 113–116, 119–131,
    136–137
revisionists, 134
Reynolds (captain), 91
Rich, Henry. *See* Holland
Riley, Theophilus, 46–50
Rodrigues Robles, Antonio, 109
Roman resolution, 4–5, 56, 119–131, 140
Roundheads, 3, 133–134, 134, 137; during
    economist period, 67–70; Roman
    resolution influenced by, 120; during
    Royalist period, 42–43, 46–50; during
    trappaner period, 77. *See also*
    Independents; Presbyterians
Royalist period, 39–50
Royalists, 3, 39–50, 134, 136–137; during
    anti-Semitic period, 112–113; during
    economist period, 53–55, 61–62, 64,
    72n3; during republican period, 87, 89,
    96, 102; Roman resolution influenced
    by, 119–131; during trappaner period,
    77, 78, 82, 83–84
Royal Mint: during anti-Semitic period,
    105–116; during economist period,
    63–64, 65, 66–67; during goldsmith
    period, 10; during republican period,
    87–102; Roman resolution influenced
    by, 124–125, 128; during Royalist
    period, 43–44, 49–50; during spy
    period, 27–28, 30; during trappaner
    period, 75–85
Rump Parliament, 102, 112, 117n25, 123

St. George, 87–102, 122–124, 135

St. Katharine Creechurch parish, 10, 20n1,
    114, 130, 138, 142
St. Paul's Cathedral, 114
St. Salvador, 87–102, 122–124, 135
Samson, 87–102, 122–124, 135
Sanlucar, Spain, 90–91
Scotland, 64–65, 68, 77, 80–81, 83,
    112–113
Scots, 39–44, 47–48, 57, 61–62, 134
Secretary of State. *See* Coke, John
Seventeenth-Century Economic Documents
    (Thirsk and Cooper), 74n54
shaving. *See* clipping
Shinner, Chris, 89
Ship Money, 40
ships, 87–102, 122–124, 135
shopkeepers, 65
Short Parliament, 41, 43
Shrewsbury, England, 100–101
Silk Office, 35–36
silver. *See specific topics*
sister, 51n30
Smart, Ithiel, 77
Smith, Adam, 5
Smith, Paul, 122–124, 131
smuggling, 90–102
Solemn League and Covenant, 47–48
Spain, 69–70, 90–91, 93–95, 96–97, 107,
    122
Spanish, 4, 137–138; ambassador, 94; in
    anti-Semitic period, 106–109, 115–116;
    during economist period, 57, 63–64, 65,
    69–70; House of Commons went to by,
    94; Netherlands, 9; during republican
    period, 87, 90–102; during Royalist
    period, 43–44, 45; during trappaner
    period, 76
spying. *See specific topics*
spy period, 23–36
Staffordshire county, 75, 77
Staneir, Jacomo, 71, 91
Star Chamber, 15–18
Steneer, James (Stenirs, James), 71, 91,
    91–92, 94
Strafford (earl), 42
Strickland, 126
suicide, 1, 3, 4–5, 139–142, 143n17; in
    essay, 129, 130–131; during goldsmith
    period, 17; spy period influenced by,

23, 36. *See also* Roman resolution
Symonds, Joseph, 28–29, 31–33, 34, 141
Symonds, William, 28–29, 31–33, 34, 141

taxes, 44–49, 66, 89, 120, 139
tax farmers, 35–36
Thirsk, Joan, 74n54
Thirty Years' War, 58–59, 63–64
Tilbury Hope, England, 91
"Tom Violet," 54
torture, 16–17
Tower of London, 10, 50, 78, 111, 134;
    economist period in, 53–61, 69, 73n5;
    during republican period, 96, 98;
    Roman resolution influenced by, 121,
    123, 128
trade, 5–6, 79–83, 106–112, 115–116,
    124–125, 138; during economist period,
    56–61, 63–64, 64–67, 68–72; during
    goldsmith period, 12–14, 15–17, 19–20;
    Jews influencing, 106–112, 115–116;
    during republican period, 87–88,
    90–102; during Royalist period, 40–41,
    43–44, 51n23; spy, 23–36. *See also* free
    trade
traitors, 123–124, 127
trappaner, 75–85, 85n1
treason, 45–50, 123–124, 127
treasure ships, 87–102, 122–124, 135
Tromp, Martin, 88–89
troy ounce, 85n12
*A True Discovery to the Commons of
    England* (Violet), 67–68, 79–80
A True Narrative of Som [*sic*] *Remarkable
    Proceedings* (Violet), 100
Turkey Company, 60, 70
Tyrell, Thomas, 114

value of £1 000, 21n10

Vane, Henry, 123
Violet, Sara. *See* Vyolett, Sara
Violet, Thomas. *See specific topics*
Virginia Company, 59
Vyolett, Peter, 9–10, 20n1
Vyolett, Sara, 2, 9, 17, 20n1, 50, 129

Walker, Walter, 91, 92, 93–94, 96
Watkins, David, 49
Watkins, Mr., 94
The Wealth of Nations (Smith, A.), 5
Welsh, 137
Welsted, Leonard, 30–31
whale blubber, 60
Whig model, 133–134
Whitaker, 120
Whitehall, 97, 108–109
will, 128, 130, 131, 140–141
Windsor, England, 128
wire drawers, 14–15, 28–36, 44, 75–85,
    121, 126; during economist period,
    60–61, 68; during republican period,
    99, 102
Wollaston, Edward, 75
Wollaston, Elizabeth, 75
Wollaston, John, 75–85, 87, 98, 141;
    during economist period, 60, 66, 68;
    during Royalist period, 45, 49–50;
    during spy period, 24, 29
Wollaston, Rebecca, 75, 77
Worcester, England, 62
World War II (WWII), 130
Worsley, Benjamin, 70, 71, 71–72
Wortley, Francis, 54
Wren, Christopher, 142
WWII. *See* World War II

xenophobia, 47–48, 70, 88, 137–138

About the Author

Amos Tubb is the Gordon B. Davidson Associate Professor of History at Centre College, where he has taught since 2005. A specialist in early modern British history, Tubb studied history as an undergraduate at the University of California, Davis, and did his graduate work at the University of California, Riverside. His publications have hitherto focused on the intersection of politics and print in Civil War–era England. Teaching at Centre College inspired Tubb to write a book aimed at an undergraduate audience, and *Thomas Violet, a Sly and Dangerous Fellow* is the result.